MW01031397

Lead Pastor

By Joe Humrichous

Shepherds
Publishing

Lead Pastor

This book, or parts thereof, may not be reproduced in any form without permission. The scanning, uploading and distribution of this book via the internet or any other means without the permission of the publisher is illegal and punishable by law. Please do not encourage or participate in any form of piracy of copyrighted materials. Your support of the author's rights is appreciated.

Please note that all scripture quotes come from the authorized King James Version unless otherwise indicated.

ISBN: 979-8-62728-903-8

Shepherds Publishing
515 6th St., P.O. Box 267
Covington, IN 47932
765-793-2177
shepherdspublishing.com
shepherdspublishing@yahoo.com
Shepherds Publishing on Facebook

Cover layout/design by:
    Sunny Wilderman

Book layout/design by:
    Word Services Unlimited
    loralee@wordservicesunlimited.com
    wordservicesunlimited.com

Printed in the United States of America.

Table of Contents

Foreword

Pastors who have experienced the emptiness of attempting to build the church in the arm of the flesh are best able to help those who are in the midst of the same discouraging dilemma. When Christ is not acknowledged as the Head of the church all methods and programs end only in fruitlessness and frustration. The responsibility of properly shepherding the flock is difficult enough when the pastor is committed to maintaining an intimacy with Christ, but it is impossible when abiding in the Vine is compromised.

The reader will appreciate how the author transparently shares from many years of experience the journey from self-focused, flesh-driven ministry to the freedom of serving with the Lord Jesus Christ as the Head of His body, the church.

In his book, *LEAD PASTOR*, Joe Humrichous addressed the most fundamental Biblical truths that keep the proper priorities in place while building the church. The recurring theme and the controlling principle is "JESUS CHRIST OBVIOUSLY PRESENT AND ACTIVELY IN CHARGE." Life changing insights will be gained by a careful study of each chapter.

The Biblical content of each chapter is a refreshing reminder to me to keep abiding in the Vine and to recognize the Lord Jesus Christ as the Head of His body, the church, which Paul calls the church of the living God and the pillar and ground of the truth. I was also reminded that being transformed into the image of Christ is a marathon, not a sprint.

LEAD PASTOR is a book that will transform a stagnant, local church into a vibrant body of joyful, fruitful believers.

Dr. Les Ollila

Dedication

To my life-long ministry friend, David Rowland.

Solomon writes about the value of a friend in Ecclesiastes 4:9-12. He starts with "Two are better than one, …" and ends with, "a threefold cord is not quickly broken." He makes it clear that both help and warmth comes to those whose lives are woven together and that they will have a good reward for their labor.

For almost 50 years we have joined hearts in kingdom work. With Dave, there was never a question about character or competence and through the oneness of the Holy Spirit God gave the chemistry of total trust and enjoyment.

As a friend, my life has been sharpened (Proverbs 27:17) by his faithful wounds (Proverbs 27:6) and sweet hearty counsel (Proverbs 27:10). I am more like Jesus because of my friend David Rowland.

As a passionate servant he gave when he had little to give and worked when there was little strength—all with no hand-out or strings attached. This is true greatness in the kingdom (Matthew 20:25) and I have been the beneficiary.

Sincerely in Christ's Love,

Joe

Acknowledgments

To Judy Rennaker, my faithful friend, prayer warrior, and encouraging administrative assistant who takes my very raw products, applies her magic and turns them into something readable. I am eternally grateful.

To my bride Teresa who not only cheers me on but challenges my thinking and catches my typos. I love you.

To my comrades at First Baptist Covington, Indiana-- pastors, staff and beloved family who pray, talk shop and give me a place to call home. A special thanks to Mike Hohenstein who helped with this manuscript and Sunny Wilderman who applied her gifts to the artwork.

To our financial supporters who help us to get the word of God to the souls of men.

To Loralee at Word Services Unlimited who takes the manuscript to the finish.

How to Use This Book

- Refresh yourself with these ideas that partially define the Christ-Church relationship. (One thought each day for 30 days.)

- Relate them to your leadership and congregation in creative ways.

- Review them as regularly as needed for ongoing discipleship and leadership training.

- 30 ideas over 30 weeks would be a good start in nurturing the Christ-life as church-life.

- Simultaneously develop a growing prayer strategy that will support the whole ministry. (Make it delightful according to Revelation 3:20—like a working breakfast, lunch or dinner.)

> Look for grace,
> Joe

Lead Pastor Introduction

Dear Shepherd,

My simple agenda in sharing the thoughts in this material is to discuss the idea of Jesus Christ obviously present and actively in charge of the local church. In this project I give 30 reasons why Jesus is the active Head of the church and thus 30 reasons why we should meet with Him together in prayer.

Leading a local church is not hard, it is impossible! All too often we rely on strong and beautiful personalities, financial resources, education or experience as the way great ministries are developed. God has given Christ alone as the way to ministry fullness (Ephesians 1:22, 23). The mystery—reality of Christ in us is our only hope of real glory.

The church is a living organism with Christ as her life. He is her active head by which she increases with the increase of God (Colossians 2:19). He is her only authority by which we overcome principalities and powers and make disciples (Matthew 28:18), her foundation on which we build (I Corinthians 3:11), her true vine in whom we abide and bear fruit (John 15:1), and her paraklete (John 14:16) through the gracious and powerful Holy Spirit.

The church is not an orphan (John 14:18); she is a bride on her way to a spotless presentation to Christ by Christ! (Ephesians 5:27) This too is a divine mystery (Ephesians 5:32). Therefore, we conclude that **Church life is Christ life**.

While in seminary, I heard for the first time the statement, "Everything rises and falls on leadership." I took it to heart, tried diligently to put it in practice and crashed and burned. Sadly, I took the credit for the good stuff and the blame for the bad stuff and became a basket-case.

Hitting the wall forced me to seek the Lord and find a new way to live. This handbook is a record of what I learned.

I still believe strongly in good leadership that sets a standard biblically, moves forward strategically, all with a gracious and loving attitude of joy. But our leadership must be put forth with a "you follow me as I follow Christ" attitude. He is the lead pastor.

Expectations

Congregations have expectations of pastors and pastors have expectations of their congregations. Each one with good intention at times painfully launch their strong opinions at each other about what can make their church great. Often these ideas center around their personal giftedness like serving, teaching, showing mercy, administration or evangelism.

Complaints swirl around the pastor needing to spend more time in the study or visiting in the homes or being a better administrator or counsellor. In turn the pastor is hoping the flock will give or serve or witness more.

While all the expectation—tension hangs in the air, no one seems to start in the right place—abiding in Jesus present and in charge. His soft knock for a dinner invitation is missed in the noise of expectation. The most common problem of an ailing congregation is Defective Abiding.

The way a church thinks is strategic to how a church lives. This series simply sets forth 30 biblical thoughts about

Christ and the local church that will allow the pastor and people to engage Jesus as LEAD pastor while still maintaining responsible human leadership.

> *"The most common problem of an ailing congregation is Defective Abiding. The way a church thinks is strategic to how a church lives."*

Only Jesus can build a church that has the power to advance the Kingdom in a pagan culture. Without Him we can do nothing. We are not manufacturers, but we can be distributors of His divine life and resources. Let's begin with the foundation.

Channels only,

Joe

Channels only, blessed Master
But with all thy wondrous power
Flowing through us,
Thou canst use us
Every day and every hour

๛ Section 1 ๙

No Other Foundation

Dear Shepherd,

The quiet thief of the church is <u>defective abiding</u>. So, give all diligence to perfect the abiding spirit of your flock.

If we choose not to embrace our union with Christ and remain in it, our church will be dry, parched and barren.

If we choose in faith to embrace our union with Him in death and resurrection and remain in Him, our church will issue fresh floods of living Water from the Spirit of God. Always remember Jesus is eager to be the Life of His church.

Abide in Me, and I in you

Reality #1—Think Biblically

All scripture is given by inspiration of God, and is profitable for doctrine, for reproof, for correction, for instruction in righteousness that the man of God may be perfect, thoroughly furnished unto all good works. –II Timothy 3:16-17

When our pastor, Andy Harkleroad, came to our church, he came with a sentence that underscored and defined his whole life and ministry. Here it is, "We must think biblically if we are going to live godly." That Bible-based agenda was modeled in the way he lived, did family, taught, preached and shepherded.

Thinking biblically seems like a given, but truth is in the busyness of ministry and in the heat of the battle we forget. In the flurry of body life, the church can often substitute thinking emotionally, traditionally, denominationally, preferentially, politically, humanly, selfishly and/or organizationally for

"Every church must develop chapter and verse eyes for its ministry." thinking biblically. Every church must develop chapter and verse eyes for its ministry.

The foundation for allowing Jesus to lead our churches must be laid with the objective truth of God's Word. A church that is built on the Son of God (I Corinthians 3:11) by the Son of God (Matthew 16:18) will be the pillar and ground of the Word of God (I Timothy 3:15), which dictates how the people of God are to behave in the house of God.

The Bible is clear, we are what we think (Proverbs 23:7). The adage, "We may not be what we think we are, but what we think—we are" is true. Many churches have been divided by "stinkin-thinkin." Jesus makes it clear with His direct statement to the Pharisees, "For out of the abundance of the heart the mouth speaks" (Matthew 12:34). And Paul instructs the church at Rome that the way to move from conformation to the world to transformation in Christ is by the renewing of the mind (Romans 12:2). So, let the church be a thinking church. Think God's Word. Think God's will. Think God's ways.

Sometimes as we look back over church history and the history of our own ministries, we sadly have to say, "What were we thinking?" But here is hope if thinking is changed, minds are renewed, and repentance becomes a lifestyle for the people of God.

Preach the Word

Following Timothy's admonition about the Word itself, he was charged to preach the Word, "I charge you therefore before God and the Lord Jesus Christ, who will judge the living and the dead at His appearing and His Kingdom: Preach the Word!

Be ready in season and out of season. Convince, rebuke, exhort with all longsuffering and teaching" (II Timothy 4:1-2).

Timothy was commanded to:
Preach
Preach the Word
Preach the Word urgently—forcefully (like a soldier going to battle)
Preach the Word constantly (no matter the environment)
Preach the Word convincingly—encouragingly—patiently—instructively.

All of this is to be done publicly before the congregation and before God who is always evaluating our preaching ministry. For me, this truth is both frightening and invigorating, but it must be done.

Learning to preach the Word as a worship to an audience of ONE (God) who will then break it, bless it, and feed the sheep, is a task to be mastered by waiting on God, in His presence while pouring over a text. But preach we must.

Remember we are feeding Jesus' sheep with Jesus' Word so they will have Jesus' mind (Philippians 2:5) and think Jesus' thoughts (I Corinthians 2:16).

Let me share Haddon Robinson's definition of expository preaching here. "Expository preaching is the communication of a biblical concept, derived from and transmitted through a historical, grammatical, and literary study of a passage in its context, which the Holy Spirit first applies to the personality and experience of the preacher, then through him to his hearers." (*Biblical Preaching*, pg. 20) In this definition, the

"Be encouraged; when people are in the Word, Jesus is in the lead."

passage governs the sermon and the power to live the text is found in the text. And, of course, context is everything. A case can easily be made that this framework for sermonizing is a most effective way to develop a biblically thinking flock.

After the Word is preached, many other approaches can and should be employed in order to nurture the Word amongst the flock. Teaching sessions, discussion groups, one-on-one discipleship, Bible studies, etc. can all be used to help develop a biblically minded people. Knowing who they are in Christ, who Christ is in them, and how to nurture that relationship as a group is especially strategic for them to be a healthy church.

Be patient, everyone who comes to Christ has started their lives with a nature that is rebellious and autonomous and must be convicted and taught by the Holy Spirit. God's truth and God's Spirit in time will alter and strengthen their attitudes and beliefs toward God, His Word, and other individuals, resulting in their lives being transformed into the image of Christ. This is a marathon not a sprint.

Truly He who has begun a good work in us will perform it until the day of Jesus Christ and we are agents of truth to build a people of truth. Be encouraged; when people are in the Word, Jesus is in the lead.

Effective and Defective Abiding

Effective abiding happens when the under shepherd is intentional in leading his leaders and the flock in cultivating the vine-branch relationship (John 15). It is not automatic. Remaining in Christ in a love relationship demands worship, meditation on God's Word, prayer, sacrifice and service.

Defective abiding allows the body to drift through neglect which allows sin diseases to creep in, distractions of nonessentials to take center stage and divisions to grieve the oneness of God's Holy Spirit.

This is the mystery—marriage of Christ and the church (Ephesians 5:32) and the intimacy between the two is a sacred stewardship to be cherished by human leaders.

Reality #2—Think Sufficiency

Beware lest any man spoil you through philosophy and vain deceit, after the tradition of men, after the rudiments of the world, and not after Christ. For in him dwelleth all the fullness of the Godhead bodily. And ye are complete in him, which is the head of all principality and power: –Colossians 2:8-1

Every true believer learns through the ups and downs of our "earth-suit" existence that our spiritual formation to Christlikeness takes a lifetime and will ultimately usher us into the glorious presence of Christ where we will see Him as He is (I John 3:2). This hope has a purifying effect on us.

Through it all however, there are turning points along the way where we see a little more of Him than we had seen before. Paul actually prayed for the Ephesian church, that they would be given by God the spirit of wisdom and revelation in the knowledge of Him—and that their spiritual eyes would see their riches in Christ (Ephesians 1:15-23). Sometimes those "eye-openers" come in the form of a sentence which changes our lives forever. Here's one of mine, "Jesus Christ obviously present and actively in charge." Here's the story.

By the time I heard this I had been teaching and pastoring for 22 years. God had graciously helped me understand my union with Christ for personal victory, and we had experienced a great deal of reviving in our church. We wanted to become a praying church and had scheduled a speaker to speak on the subject of prayer to help us. A few days before the meeting, I called to get

"Joe, I'm going to speak on Jesus Christ obviously present and actively in charge."

his message titles in order to inform our people. His name was Oliver Price from Dallas, Texas. Oliver said, "Joe, I'm going to speak on Jesus Christ obviously present and actively in charge."

When he said that, my whole world focused! It was like all the lenses of my spiritual camera focused. Everything I needed for life—home—and church became defined for me in these eight words.

- Revival happens here.
- Wretched circumstances are confronted here.
- Pathetic relationships are healed here.
- Spiritual authority is found here.
- Graced-filled enablement flows from here.

Clearly this is nothing other than what we believe as the sufficiency of Christ. And I'm speaking to the ordinary pastor, who like me, is in the trenches, engaged in hand-to-hand combat for the power of the gospel and the glory of God. We and our church must think "sufficiency".

We must not reveal our wavering hearts with worrisome words like, "I know Jesus will build His church, but... !? Often what we say after the but betrays what we believe and gives us a sort of illegitimate permission to look for other saviors.

So, let's take a sort of sufficiency inventory Remember our title:

Jesus Christ Obviously Present and Actively in Charge
Ask yourself:

- Is there any need in any church of any size in any place that this biblical reality doesn't supply?

- What is the only limitation to this truth?
- Should we not start here and stay here and end here?
- Are we totally immersed in believing the supernatural sufficiency of Christ and His Word to build His church?
- Do we know how to bring His sufficiency to the forefront in our leadership practically?

If Christ is to be in the lead, then He must be believed and received in both His authority and in His sufficiency.

I love John Stotts statement that the centrality of the gospel will determine the circumference of the gospel. I would add that the sufficiency of the person of Jesus Christ must be the centrality of the gospel or else we have nothing at all. Nothing is more deadening to a church than the constant busy dealing with the outer shell of lifeless religion. So, think—at all times—sufficiency.

Reality #3—Think Organically

God is faithful by whom ye were called unto the fellowship of His Son, Jesus Christ our Lord. –I Corinthians 1:9

Therefore let no man glory in men. For all things are yours. Whether Paul or Apollos or Cephas, or the world or life or death, or things present or things to come—all are yours, and ye are Christ's and Christ is God's. –I Corinthians 3:21-23

Where do you start when you take on a tough church riddled with multiple problems? If you were a church consultant in Corinth, what would you say first? After the Apostle's greeting and thanksgiving for their gifts he reminded them of the core calling at the center of their existence… "You were called into the fellowship of His Son Jesus Christ our Lord." Corinth had proud attitudes and permissive actions because they forgot who was to be the center of their fellowship and the source of their fruitfulness. They had also made their shepherds into celebrities and chosen their favorites hoping for the success that great leadership brings.

Again, Paul points out, "All are yours, and you are Christ's and Christ is God's." I love to relate to a church, small or large, that if they have Jesus, they have everything they need to be all that God intended for them to be. Corinth had forgotten that the Life of Jesus was the life of their church.

Thinking organically gets lost in our quest for speedy results, but to understand it and practice it allows us as a church to bear our fruit in our seasons and establish a root system which stabilizes and nourishes the body season after season.

To think organically is to know that the **Life within (Christ) must become the life without (Christlikeness)**, and that He is intimately available to become in us all that He expects out of us! The most important part of church life is its spiritual root system that draws on the hidden resources we have in Christ (Colossians 2:7). The number one problem with most churches is what I have identified as Defective Abiding. We have ignored the root system and have looked to man-made cisterns that are broken and can hold no water.

Also, fruit is not the same as "results" because fruit has in it the seed for more fruit. Fruit comes from life, the life of God flowing in and through us by the Holy Spirit. Let's consider four organic images in scripture which help us understand life within becoming the life without.

The Seed

Having grown up on a farm, I learned first-hand the value of good seed. I also learned that every little seed had to die if we were to have a crop.

The mystery of Christ in us, the hope of glory (Colossians 1:27), is the seed. His presence in us is the hope of future glory for the church and the hope of present glory in the church. As we decrease, He must increase" (John 3:30). The results are glorious. This is where dying becomes living (John 12:24) and our lives are replaced by His.

The Head

Head and body verses describing Christ and the church also convey the idea of an organism. As the physical body cannot live without the head, neither can a church live without a healthy connection with her head (Ephesians 4:15, 16). We

"To think organically is to know that the Life within (Christ) must become the life without (Christlikeness)." are instructed to be "holding fast to the Head from whom all the body nourished and knit together by joints and ligaments, grows with the increase that is from God" (Colossians 2:19).

Here the Head (Christ) nourishes the believing body with His life and increases in shape and size according to His design. This is another organic reality. The key here is to have the body carefully attend to the prayer connection and submission to the Head. There is no spiritual growth for the body apart from union with the Head, Christ. Our lives are nourished by His.

Metamorphosis

This is the supernatural process where our lives are transformed by His. Think about the process of a butterfly transforming to a caterpillar, then back to a butterfly. I love this verse, "But we all with unveiled face, beholding as in a mirror the glory of the Lord, are being transformed into the same image from glory to glory, just as by the Spirit of the Lord" (II Corinthians 3:18).

This is where "beholding" is "becoming." Here we learn that the church looks like what it looks at. We are transformed into His image as we gaze into His life in His word. Therefore, let the church have no other fascination.

The Vine

No doubt one of the best descriptions of the organic nature of the relationship between believers and Jesus is the passage *"…the church worships Christ and serves Christ like Christ out of the riches of Christ."*

13

"...the church looks like what it looks at."

describing the Vine and the branches in John 15 "I am the Vine," you are the branches. He who abides in Me and I in him, bears much fruit; for without Me you can do nothing." In this illustration, our lives bear fruit through His and abiding becomes fruitfulness. Everything we dream of for our church is found here. Fruit, more fruit, much fruit, lasting fruit, friendship with Christ, fullness of joy, and powerful praying flow from effective abiding. (Remember, earlier I said, "defective abiding is the problem.")

This is the opposite of how we think and by its very nature demands our undivided attention because Jesus said, "Without Me you can do nothing." There is no other way.

Conclusion

As we learn to think organically and let Jesus lead out of the presence of His life, we need to ask:

1. How does this effect my leadership concerns?
2. How does this regulate ministry priorities, functions, and structures?
3. Does this say something about regenerate church membership?
4. Where does evangelism fit in the organic idea?

Simply remember the church worships Christ and serves Christ like Christ out of the riches of Christ. That's thinking organically.

∝ Section 2 ∾
The Praying Church

Lead Pastor

Dear Shepherd,

Transforming gospel prayer is when believers pray God's truth into their lives—agreeing together with humble repentant hearts.

Give all diligence to put prayer in its place and do your best to make prayer meetings life-giving.

We know prayer is important. Let's work hard at making it available, effective and satisfying. Many venues in smaller cells could also facilitate a broader involvement.

One heart—One soul—Great grace

Reality #4—Prayer–The Place to Start

I exhort therefore, that, first of all supplications, prayers, intercessions, and giving of thanks be made for all men.
–I Timothy 2:1

Every good leader will embody some ambition, or he probably won't be a good leader. But if Jesus is the lead pastor, our leadership must start with prayer.

In the language of the Bible Paul instructed Timothy to "pray first." Literally he said, "Before all your doings…pray." Evidently the Ephesian church had stopped praying and Paul urged Timothy to make it a priority again. Where we start will set a trajectory for where we go and where we end up. Where we start can also be a protection for wrong motives as well as fleshly methods. Timothy was a God-called man who was

"But if Jesus is the lead pastor, our leadership must start with prayer."

"Where we start will set a trajectory for where we go and where we end up."

getting marching orders in how to wage a good warfare (1:18) and avoid shipwreck in his life and leadership (1:19).

Give Jesus the first appointment of the day and of the work week. Let the first strategy be a prayer strategy which will provide a base of operation for everything else in the church. Build scripture praying by Spirit-filled believers into the foundation of ministry so that the superstructure of ministry won't collapse because of a lack of support.

Jesus has a will, a word, and a way for our church, and we will know it if we slow down and pray until He clearly reveals it to us. Take time with a few spirit-filled believers to develop an undergirding of prayer before you do anything else. Let your ministry be birthed by God. If we are going to have effective outreach, we must have fervent and effectual upreach. Strategic outreach is given its grace through strategically timed upreach in prayer.

The early church "waited for the Promise of the Father" (Acts 1:4) and "continued with one accord in prayer" (Acts 1:14). So, "when the Day of Pentecost had fully come, they were all with one accord in one place" (Acts 2:1). Being obedient in prayer first put them right where they needed to be in order to strategically launch their witness. They didn't plan their birth; God birthed His plan for them, and it was perfect.

Through praying first, we will stay in touch which then allows us to stay in tune with Jesus all the time—and that's where all fruitful ministry begins. Make these times of prayer joyful, focused and expectant. Savor them by grace and not laborious grudge. God is for us. He is our #1 cheerleader.

From Belief to Behavior:

No one can prescribe what the prayer strategy for your situation should be. But here is a suggestion: Pray, then choose two spirit-filled believers from within your ministry who will pray with you about a prayer strategy for your church. Keep it simple, scriptural, and spirit-filled; i.e. life giving. Re-evaluate the prayer life of your church or ministry on a regular basis as it grows and changes—as Jesus leads and builds His church.

Reality #5—Pray the Word

All Scripture [is] given by inspiration of God, and [is] profitable for doctrine, for reproof, for correction, for instruction in righteousness, that the man of God may be perfect, thoroughly equipped unto all good works. –II Timothy 3:16, 17

We are about to look into the reality of allowing the Word of God to provide the framework of our thoughts when we pray. I have found that many avoid public prayer meetings of any kind because they have the notion that in some way they need to be eloquent like some aged saint. Sadly, at times we can give the impression that praying somehow is a bit of a speech contest. Nothing could be further from the truth and we must let Jesus take them by the hand and give them His words to pray back to Him. When the child of God repeats the Word of God back to God, the Spirit of God prays through the Son of God and he is heard because he is praying in the will of God (I John 5:14).

The Great Benefits of Praying the Word of God

The main method of prayer in the fight for joy is to pray the Word of God. That is, to read or recite the Word and turn it into prayer as you go. Most people (certainly including me) do not have the power of mind to look at nothing and yet offer up to God significant spiritual desires for any length of time. I suspect this has always been the case. To pray for longer than a few minutes in a God-centered, Christ-exalting way requires the help of God's Spirit, and the Spirit loves to help by the Word he inspired.

This is the central method of prayer that I believe most earnest Christians have discovered: "to meditate on the Word of God… turning all, as I go into prayer." Someone may ask "How can I spend an hour in prayer? I'm done asking for what I need in five or ten minutes." I answer: Take a passage of Scripture and start reading it slowly. After each sentence, pause and go back and turn what you read into prayer. In this way you can pray as long as you can read. You may pray all day.[1]

Here are some points to consider as we pray on the foundation of objective truth.

- Rescue prayer from being only a monologue of human thoughts.
- Participate with God in His Word.
- Prayer will always be boring if it is only a monologue.
- We pray best with our Bibles open.
- We can be transformed in the place of prayer.
- Scripture meditation can be considered praying.
  (Joshua 1:8; Psalm 1:1-3; Jeremiah 15:16)

Oswald Chambers in his book, *If You Will Ask*, says "The purpose of prayer is not to get healed, get a job, get our house sold, or get whatever else we want. It is to get the life of God in us. Prayer does not change things, it changes me, and then I change things."[2]

Consider the influence of two simple, straight forward scriptures.

"We pray best with our Bibles open."

One thing I have desired of the LORD, that will I seek: That I may dwell in the house of the LORD all the days of my life, to behold the beauty of the LORD, and to inquire in His temple. –Psalm 27:4 NKJV

But we all, with unveiled face, beholding as in a mirror the glory of the Lord, are being transformed into the same image from glory to glory, just as by the Spirit of the Lord. –II Corinthians 3:18 NKJV

We look like what we look at, or as some would say, "We become what we behold." That's how prayer works on an individual and corporate level. That's how prayer works. Warren Wiersbe said it well.

When the child of God looks into the Word of God and sees the Son of God, he is changed by the Spirit of God into the image of God for the glory of God.

Transforming Gospel Prayer

Transforming gospel prayer is when believers pray God's truth into their lives—agreeing together with humble repentant hearts.

From Belief to Behavior

Martin Luther's pattern for prayer scripture:

Look for instruction:
"Lord, I see here that . . . "

Give thanks:
"Thank you . . . "

Confess (If applicable)
"Lord, I confess . . . "

Prayer, Intercession, Application:
"Lord that makes me think of . . . "
(Other references. people, circumstances. situations)

Nurturing the Vine-branch Relationship

Remember: Praying in agreement with Scripture nurtures the Life of Christ within and allows us to develop a strong root system and fruitful life. (Psalms 1:1-3; John 15:1-16; Colossians 2:6,7)

Reality #6—Pray God's Character

For of Him and through Him and to Him are all things, to whom be glory forever. Amen –Romans 11:36

One year our church was starting a series of meetings in which we were praying and hoping for a reviving. On the first Sunday of the meeting the well-known veteran revivalist announced his sermon title. He said today we are going to learn where revival begins. I thought, "Oh great, here we go again. I know what he's going to say—I've heard this before." You know the idea of draw a circle and get in it and let revival begin with me. Honestly, I didn't want anything else to have to begin with me.

To my joyful surprise the speaker said something I had never heard before! He said, "A revival that begins in the character of God is as a river ever deepening and widening until it falls into the expanse of God's great eternity. I immediately felt relief and blessed to know that our effort for a reviving started in the right place. The same is true with effectual prayer. Jesus' leadership will always have us start with the character of God.

Pray in God's Holy Character

True religion confronts earth with heaven and brings eternity to bear upon time. The Church has surrendered her once lofty concept of God and has substituted for it one so low, so ignoble, as to be utterly unworthy of things, worshiping men. The low view of God entertained

> *"Jesus' leadership will always have us start with the character of God."*

almost universally among Christians is the cause of a hundred lesser evils everywhere among us.

"What comes into our minds when we think about God is the most important thing about us."

With our loss of the sense of the majesty has come the further loss of religious awe and consciousness of the divine Presence. It is impossible to keep our moral practices sound and our inward attitudes right while our idea of God is erroneous or inadequate.

What comes into our minds when we think about God is the most important thing about us. Worship is pure or base as the worshiper entertains high or low thoughts of God. We tend by a secret law of the soul to move toward our mental image of God. This is true not only of the individual Christian, but of the company of Christians that composes the Church. Compared with our actual thoughts about Him, our creedal statements are of little consequence. I believe there is scarcely an error in doctrine or a failure in applying Christian ethics that cannot be traced finally to imperfect and ignoble thoughts about God. Low views of God destroy the gospel for all who hold them.

A god begotten in the shadows of a fallen heart will quite naturally be no true likeness of the true God. "Thou thoughtest," said the Lord to the wicked man in the psalm, "that I was altogether such as one as thyself." The essence of idolatry is the entertainment of thoughts about God that are unworthy of Him.

The heaviest obligation lying upon the Christian Church today is to purify and elevate her concept of God until it is once more worthy of Him—and of her. In all her prayers and labors this should have first place.[3] –A.W. Tozer

- Here we are learning to pray within the boundaries of the character and activity of God.
- Here we will rescue prayer from not being heard.
- We will participate with God's heart for all things.
- Here we can pray with confidence.

Now this is the confidence we have in Him, that if we ask anything according to His will, He hears us. And if we know that He hears us, whatever we ask, we know that we have the petitions that we have asked of Him. –I John 5:14-15 NKJV

Are we imitating a religious practice or participating with the Living God?

Is a proper request important?

Who helps us?

Likewise, the Spirit also helps in our weaknesses. For we do not know what we should pray for as we ought, but the Spirit Himself makes intercession for us with groanings which cannot be uttered. Now He who searches the hearts knows what the mind of the Spirit is, because He makes intercession for the saints according to the will of God. –Romans 8:26, 27 NKJV

Our Lord left us a perfect template for all praying that considered God's character.

In this manner, therefore, pray:

Our Father in heaven, Hallowed be Your name
Your kingdom come.
Your will be done
On earth as it is in heaven.
Give us this day our daily bread.

And forgive us our debts,
As we forgive our debtors.
And do not lead us into temptation,
But deliver us from the evil one.
For Yours is the kingdom and the power and the glory
forever. Amen –Matthew 6:9-13 NKJV

The disciples considered God's omniscience between the ascension and Pentecost.

You, O Lord, who knows the hearts of all, show which of these two you have chosen to take part in this ministry and apostleship from which Judas by transgression fell, that he might go to his own place. –Acts 1:24-25 NKJV

There is a place of infinite power and authority and we as a congregation need to unite there.

A Place:
- Where God is glorified
- Where Jesus is prized
- Where the Spirit is obeyed
- Where Scripture is the prayer list
- Where faith is the life-line
- Where repentance is the lifestyle
- Where believers agree as one
- Where group praying is the format

From Belief to Behavior
- Isolate the need
- Match the need with one or more aspects of God's character

- Match the need with one or more of God's names.
- Support with appropriate scripture
- Turn to God and pray
- Rejoice in being heard

Reality #7—Pray the Cross

From whence come wars and fightings among you? Come they not hence, even of your lusts that war in your members? Ye lust, and have not: ye kill, and desire to have, and cannot obtain: ye fight and war, yet ye have not, because ye ask not. Ye ask and receive not, because ye ask amiss, that ye may consume it upon your lusts.
—James 4:1-3

Here we are putting prayer at the cross. We are learning to live and pray from a cross-centered life. Needless to say, we again follow our Lead Pastor as He role-modeled this to redemptive perfection. We must rescue prayer from self-centeredness and participate in the very life of Christ. Jesus never asked anything "amiss" and the Father always heard Him. (John 11:42). He is our example and leader.

Pray at the Cross

When we come to consider prayer in the light of co-crucifixion, as this position may be called, we find that prayer truly comes into its own on this basis. Prayer is nothing if it is not communion, and true communion is only possible when the "old life" which cannot have fellowship with God is terminated.

The reason why many are finding prayer so unsatisfactory and the life of prayer so unattractive is because they have attempted to enter into the celestial realms of prayer in the strength of the "old man!"

True prayer can only be offered on the basis of *co-crucifixion.* This is the prime condition. "If you abide in Me and I in you,

> *"We must rescue prayer from self-centeredness and participate in the very life of Christ."*

you will ask what you desire, and it shall be done for you." We must be "in Christ." But we cannot be in Christ in the fullest sense unless in the power of the Savior's death *we commit to death the "old life."*

It is when we realize our oneness with Christ in death and resurrection that prayer becomes the marvelous force that we find it was in the life of the Savior, the invincible dynamic that it reveals itself to be in the book of Acts, and the ineffable experience of the great saints of the ages. It is then that our spirits will, liberated by the power of the cross from their fleshly and soulish entanglements, "mount up on wings as eagles." It is then that the communion with God comes spontaneously and naturally to its fullest expression.

Prayer then becomes a working out of the will of God, and therefore must prevail—be the difficulties what they may, however staggering the problem, however great the need. It is then that the great disparity between what the Master said prayer would accomplish and the **miserable caricature** that is in the actual practice of millions, is removed, and prayer blossoms out in all the glory of its true nature!

Seeing prayer in the light of the cross and our **participation** in the Savior's death and resurrection, we are not the least surprised over the achievements of some of the great prayer warriors of the church.[4] (Hugel)

Meditate on these scriptures for encouragement.

Most assuredly, I say to you, unless a grain of wheat falls into the ground and dies, it remains alone: but if it dies, it produces much grain. –John 12:24 NKJV

I have been crucified with Christ, it is no longer I who live, but Christ lives in me: and the life which I now live in the flesh I live by faith in the Son of God, who loved me and gave Himself for me. –Galatians 2:20 NKJV

"Are there rights you are yet clinging to?"

But God forbid that I should glory except in the cross of our Lord Jesus Christ, by whom the world has been crucified to me, and I to the world. –Galatians 6:14 NKJV

Are there rights you are yet clinging to? When we come to the cross, we lay down the weapons of a rebel and desire Christ and Christ alone. We will arrive at a place where we will confess, "I can live without anything or anyone but Jesus." I will warn you that in Jesus ministry, the closer we get to the cross—the smaller the crowd.

Therefore, put prayer at the cross.

Jesus' Model

Now my soul is troubled, and what shall I say? Father save me from this hour? But for this purpose, I came to this hour. Father, glorify your name. –John 12:27-28 NKJV

From Belief to Behavior:
- Clinging to your rights is deficient abiding. Do your prayers evidence abiding in Christ or in self?
- Jesus went from thousands on a hillside to 12 at the table, to one at the cross (John). Don't be discouraged if your prayer circle at the cross is small.

Reality #8—Pray in the Vine

I am the Vine, ye are the branches; He who abideth in Me, and I in him, the same bringeth forth much fruit; for without Me ye can do nothing. –John 15:5

It seems that most of our journeys in the service of the Lord begin with the idea that we are going to work "for" the Lord. Thus, our prayers take on a similar fashion as we try to think of something to ask Him "for." Consequently, while good-hearted, we start in the wrong place. In this reality we are going to join our Lead Pastor within His life as the True Vine. We are going to see ourselves in our true position and pray while abiding in the Vine. Here we will rescue prayer from self-sufficiency, random requests, and fruitlessness.

My view of leadership and ministry began to drastically change after my first reading of Andrew Murray's classic handbook on *The True Vine*. The Vine is the sole provider for the branch. The branch needs only to obey and abide. The care and nutrients the branch receives from the Vine are more than enough to bear all the fruit it can handle. When we in our inner man posture ourselves here, we are in a perfect place to work with Him, rest in Him and pray rightly. While we double down on doctrine we can double up on dependence and wisely double check on our methods.

> "While we double down on doctrine we can double up on dependence and wisely double check on our methods."

Veteran missionary F. J. Huegel says it this way in *Bones of His Bone*:

One thing for the missionary is inevitable. If he is to go forward in the face of seemingly insuperable obstacles which beset him, ushering in a new day for enslaved souls, there are definite spiritual requirements.

If he is to do what God expects of him, and the church expects of him, and what the heart-rending need of these to whom he is an ambassador of light requires of him, then *he must himself appropriate in an ever deeper and fuller way the power of Christ.* He must himself be bound to that unconquerable Christ who all down the centuries has through His disciples achieved the impossible. He must get beyond a mere intellectual knowledge of the historical Christ, and so entwine the tendrils of his spiritual nature in the eternal Christ that he imbibes a *divine life*!

The job he is attempting to do requires of him superhuman force. The merely human, however noble and strong and cultivated, will prove as insufficient and as inadequate as a handful of glowing coals would be for the dissipation of an arctic blizzard. He must transcend the purely natural and immerse himself in the supernatural. He must experience the power of the indwelling Christ, and, dispossessed of his own life, become in an ever-fuller measure possessed of a divine life. Our "rivers of living water" flowing from His innermost being—the promise which the Savior has made to His own—can make possible the renewal of life in those to whom he is sent.

Here are the laws of the Vine:
- The law of life in Christ alone
  "I am the Vine"
- The law of ownership
  "My Father is the vinedresser"
- The law of the cleansing Word
  "You are already clean because of the Word which I have spoken to you."

- The law of abiding
  "Abide in Me"
- The law of helplessness
  "Without Me you can do nothing."
- The law of love
  "Abide in My love."

Here are two unconditional promises about prayer as we abide in the life of our Lead Pastor:

If you abide in Me, and My words abide in you, you will ask what you desire, and it shall be done for you. –John 15:7 NKJV

You did not choose Me, but I chose you and appointed you that you should go and bear fruit, and that your fruit should remain, that whatever you ask the Father in My name, He may give you. –John 15:16 NKJV

Please notice that we have been chosen and called by Jesus to do this.

From Belief to Behavior:
- Give thanks for your place in the Vine.
- Give thanks for your calling.
- Take note of the "do nothing."
- Pray through the laws of the Vine.
- Rejoice—Remain—Rest—Reproduce

Reality #9—Pray Together with Christ

Behold I stand at the door and knock. If any man hear My voice and opens the door, I will come in to him and will sup with him, and he with Me. –Revelation 3:20

Here we are invited to pray together in our shared relationship in Jesus. Certainly, our relationship with Jesus is **personal**, but it is not **private**; it is shared.

In this reality we are participating with the body of Christ and rescuing prayer from autonomy and individualism. This is a precious and powerful opportunity for a church, and can you believe it—Jesus is actually knocking on our door in order to engage us!

My beloved mentor, Oliver Price, says it so well.

Prayer is much greater than bringing a list of requests to God. Prayer is letting Jesus Himself come into our midst to commune with us and glorify His name through meeting our needs. Our Lord's heart cry is evident in Revelation 3:20, "Behold, I stand at the door and knock. If anyone hears My voice and opens the door, I will come in to him and dine with him, and he with Me." O. Hallesby, in his classic book entitled *Prayer*, commented as follows:

I doubt that I know of a passage in the whole Bible that throws greater light upon prayer than this one does. It is, it seems to me, the key which opens the door into the holy and blessed realm of prayer.

To pray is nothing more involved than to let Jesus in on our needs. To pray is to give Jesus permission to employ

"To pray is nothing more involved than to let Jesus in on our needs."

His powers in the alleviation of our distress. To pray is to let Jesus glorify His name in the midst of our needs.[5]

Private prayer is necessary. But we also need to pray with others, striving to unite under the headship of Christ and His shepherd care. Praying with others in His presence under His active leadership is also necessary. A lady known for her fervent prayers said, "That's where the power is." Another lady commented, "We need to listen to one another's hearts in the presence of God.

Certainly, we need the power of God's Spirit breathing in and through us as we pray. Praying corporately can be structured so as to focus on the presence of Christ and unite our prayers under His life-transforming headship. The church began *not as a preaching service* with a small prayer meeting (Acts 1:14); rather, the church *was* a prayer meeting.[6]

I think we need to preserve the idea that the church was a prayer meeting designed to steward the connection between the church and Christ. That stewardship cannot effectively be done just through closet prayers. There must be a corporate dimension—and may I quickly emphasize the importance of making them life-giving! We must stop the bad habits that kill group prayer. Replace bad habits with good features. Arrange the seating for group participation. Start with a short chorus to focus hearts. Read with emphasis an appropriate scripture to tune the minds. Keep requests to a minimum. Suggest sentence prayers to maximize participation. Encourage them to pray loud enough to be heard. End with a joyful song. Many things can be done to make a prayer meeting vibrant. Be creative, simple and flexible. Meet with Jesus.

"… the church was a prayer meeting designed to steward the connection between the church and Christ."

We need to remember the church will be disconnected from prayer if prayer is disconnected from Jesus. Colossians 1:15-27 does a great job keeping the majesty of Jesus and the mystery of Jesus together. (Hint—a really good study clearly presented.) "Christ in you (plural), the hope of glory" is why we should be fully convinced that every gospel preaching church can be healthy, walk in revival, and be full of glory!

Further observations:
- All that we're longing for in the gospel community;
    Transformation of lives
    Glory in the church
    Every man perfect in Christ
    Life flowing from one living fountain, "Christ in you the hope of glory."
- The majesty of Jesus (Colossians 15-19) and the mystery of Jesus (v. 26, 27) must be kept intact.
- We are ministers and stewards of this miraculous and powerful union (v. 24, 25).
- Jesus also must have preeminence as the active head of the church (v. 18).
- All fullness (plaroma) and completeness dwells in Jesus (1:19, 2:9-10).
- His active headship ensures church increase that comes from God (Colossians 2:18-19).

These truths are "Wow" factors and should fascinate our imaginations. They are much more powerful than goals centered around human accomplishment.

From Beliefs to Behavior:
- Find Biblical titles of Jesus, and
- Pray through a few at a time together.
- Make prayer gatherings engaging ("O Jesus, please be Jesus in us.").
- Rejoice in hope because it's real!

Reality #10—Pray for Inner Man First

And the very God of peace sanctify you wholly; and I pray God your whole spirit and soul and body be preserved blameless unto the coming of our Lord Jesus Christ. – I Thessalonians 5:23

Too much of too many prayer meetings is taken up with wordy requests and rambling moans about the outer man. This would be tolerable if there was at least some effort to pray on behalf of the inner man. Sadly, we earthlings default to prayers that concentrate on "when can I get out of this rather than <u>what</u> can I get out of this." I am not heartless here. To the contrary, the scripture itself informs us, "The spirit of a man will sustain him in sickness, but who can bear a broken spirit?" (Proverbs 18:14 NKJV)

Our introductory verse above also gives direction to the truth that sanctification is perfected from the inside out. So, let's pray for the inner man first.

In reality, we want to rescue prayer from outer man needs only. This allows us to **participate** with God's work in the transformation process through the trials of faith. When we focus on the spirit of man and claim the promises of God, we become actual **partakers** of the divine nature which allows all of life to focus with a divine purpose. Therefore, let us pray for strength in the inner man.

Here's a word from the autobiography of George Mueller.

"It has pleased the Lord to teach me a truth, the benefit of which I have not lost for more than 14 years. The point is this: I saw more clearly than ever the first great and primary business to which I ought to attend every day was to have my soul happy in the Lord. The first thing to be concerned about was not how much I might serve the Lord, or how I might glorify the Lord, but how I might get my soul into a happy state, and how my inner man might be nourished.

How different, when the soul is refreshed and made happy early in the morning, from what it is when, without spiritual preparation, the service, the trials, and the temptations of the day come upon me."[7]

Our Lead Pastor illustrated this in His model prayer when He simply included, "Give us this day our daily bread." Again, we don't need to eliminate outer man needs from our praying; we just need to put it in its proper place. The Apostle Paul related the value of inner man praying this way.

For which cause we faint not: but though our outward man perish, yet the inward man is renewed day by day. For our light affliction, which is but for a moment, worketh for us a far more exceeding and eternal weight of glory, while we look not at the things which are seen, but at the things which are not seen. For the things which are seen are temporal, but the things which are not seen are eternal. –II Corinthians 4:16-18

Three of Paul's prayers stand out as examples: inner sight (Ephesians 1:15-23), inner strength (Ephesians 3:14-21), inner direction (Colossians 1:9-14).

We would be wise to note the transformational value of such praying.

Shepherds, please remember this kind of praying requires instruction, nurturing, and role modeling. Keep building your prayer core and allow them to be a

> *"Even our spirit of joy witnesses to the sufficiency of Jesus and that's contagious."*

holy leaven growing throughout the congregation. There is a huge cause here! Strength in the inner man is a universal need and has many audiences who are watching how we respond from the heart (Ephesians 3:1-21).

1) The heathen (v. 8,9)
2) The angels (v. 10)
3) The persons involved (v. 13)
4) The family of God (v. 14)
5) Jesus (v. 17)
6) All generations (the children) (v. 21)

Even our spirit of joy witnesses to the sufficiency of Jesus and that's contagious.

These things I have spoken to you, that My joy may remain in you, and that your joy may be full. –John 15:11 NKJV

From Belief to Behavior:
- Examine some key prayers from Paul. What were the requests? Consider praying them back to God also.
- Think about what "daily bread" may include. Read and pray through John 6:35-51.
- Keep physical requests in perspective.
- Give value to trials biblically.
- Wait expectantly for grace.

Reality #11—Pray in the Harvest to the Lord of the Harvest

Then saith he unto his disciples, "The harvest truly is plenteous, but the labourers are few; pray ye therefore the Lord of the harvest, that he will send forth labourers into his harvest."
–Matthew 9:37-38

Nobody knows the harvest like the Lord of the harvest, and here He gives instruction as to how we are to pray effectively for this vast, ever-needy mission. Our Lead Pastor is moved with compassion (sick to His stomach) when He sees His sheep with no shepherd. He alone sees their real condition from the heart out and knows who should reach them and how. So, He says, "Pray the Lord of the harvest". In John 4:35, He also says to the disciples, "Lift up your eyes and look at the fields." He knows if we look and pray, we will rescue prayer from becoming ingrown and participate with Him in the harvest. Remember the harvest belongs to the Lord of the harvest, i.e. The Head of your church!

Is Your Prayer Meeting Maintenance or Frontline?

A Pastor's Story:
Our prayer meeting in Pennsylvania was intended to function as a battle station, the earlier meeting in California was largely designed to maintain the existing life and ministry of our congregation. Believers came to the earlier meeting to be edified by a Bible study that took up most of the hour and to pray for the internal

needs of the church. Expectancy seemed to be at a low ebb among attenders, evidenced by the fact that none of us bothered to keep a record of prayers offered and answered. I

"Is your prayer meeting maintenance or frontline?"

also do not think that Christians came to this prayer meeting expecting to meet God in a life-changing encounter. Thus, it died.

By contrast, people came to the frontline prayer meeting to be changed. They discovered what Augustine has emphasized, that man's chief need is to fellowship with God, to find fulfillment in Him, and to experience the abiding presence of Jesus (Psalms 27:4; 36:7-9; John 14:18-23; 15:1-10). So, they came to be changed, and they were changed because Jesus kept His promise to be wherever two or three gather in His name (Matthew 19:19-20). From Him they received grace to confess and forsake their sins, to be touched with His compassion for the lost, and to go forth to "put feet on their prayers" through witnessing by words and deeds of love.

Speaking of maintenance-style prayer meetings, Steve Harper says bluntly that "they are not really prayer meetings." In his useful little book *Prayer Ministry in the Local Church*, he concludes, "They are usually Bible studies with five minutes of prayer tacked on at the end." Ours in California actually was given to prayer, but its conception and format were designed more to preserve the status quo of the inward-looking church rather than to break down its rigidities. By contrast, the frontline prayer assembly has a revolutionary purpose.

The prayer of those who attend it is summarized in the words, "Thy kingdom come."[8] –C. J. Miller

Here is a simple pattern of God's Harvest Work:
1. We become occupied with the Lord of the harvest. (Matthew 9:38)
2. He pours His life into us. (Matthew 10:1)
3. He sends us forth with our instructions. (Matthew 10:5ff)
4. We give freely what He has freely given us. (Matthew 10:8)
"When revival is the experience of the church, then evangelism will be the expression of the church."

We are participants in His harvest.

The Lord is passionate for His harvest and He has invited us to join Him starting at home in prayer.

Remember, missions exist because worship doesn't. Jesus, our lead example, obeyed the Father and went through Samaria (John 4) because His Father was seeking worshippers (v. 23). Guest what? A Samaritan woman became a true worshiper through faith in the true Messiah. The Father gained a worshiper and a lost needy woman was rescued, because Jesus marched to the beat of one drummer—His Father. So can we!

From Belief to Behavior:
- Take time to worship Jesus as Lord of the Harvest.
- Formulate the harvest in our area and families.
- Get statistics on other nations one at a time and ask the Lord what to do about it.
- Thank Him for every movement of grace.

• Say—"Here am I Lord—send me to your place for me."

"When revival is the experience of the church, then evangelism will be the expression of the church.

Lead Pastor

❧ Section 3 ☙

Attitude

Lead Pastor

Dear Shepherd,
   It has been said that the enemy of the church will be carried into the assembly on the back of human pride.
   Knowing that God resists the proud, we must give all diligence to shepherd the attitudes with truth. The cross of Christ is not only our message, it is our method.
   Lion-like victories can be won in lamb-like ways when Christ-like attitudes prevail.
   Let this mind be in you

Reality #12—Ownership— A Possession to Protect

Take heed therefore unto yourselves, and to all the flock, over the which the Holy Ghost hath made you overseers, to feed the church of God which he hath purchased with his own blood.
–Acts 20:28

There are times when defense becomes the best offense. And if Jesus is going to be the Lead Pastor, we under shepherds must diligently protect His blood-bought purchase of the church.

Only One may have preeminence in all things (Colossians 1:18). Many a church have felt the wrenching heartache, division and yes, even death caused by misplaced ownership. Pastors are shepherds not CEOs. Deacons are servants not shareholders. Congregations are sheep, not mobs that rule. Even strong and faithful families who have weathered

"Sacrifice and service is never an entitlement to ownership."

the storms of a local body for a long time can assume some ownership that is not theirs. Denominational real estate can also become a point of pride and can usurp ownership from Jesus. Sacrifice and service is never an entitlement to ownership.

While the enemy is always aggressive and strategically attempting to infiltrate a congregation from without, most of the wolves come from within.

For I know this that after my departure, savage wolves will come in among you, not sparing the flock. Also from among yourselves men will rise up speaking perverse things, to draw away the disciples after themselves. –Acts 20:29-30 NKJV

Sadly, our hearts have a tendency to love preeminence like Diotrephes (III John 9) and we become discontented servants. As we begin to talk nonsense in private counsels and public meetings, Jesus is grieved and begins to withdraw His hand and turn His face away. Another candlestick is removed.

The opposite is true of a local church that respects, guards, and stewards Christ's ownership. When we take heed and are vigilant about these matters, Jesus is free to advance His life and power and express His love amid joy throughout the congregation. This puts His life on display which in turn transforms saints and sinners for His glory. If we keep our hands on the plow but off the merchandise, we will have His best.

From Belief to Behavior:
Here's how to practice "His Ownership" in your stewardship.

> *"Occasionally, as you are led, initiate a public ceremony where everyone agrees in oneness that the church belongs to Jesus."*

1. Pray first, pray often, pray together. Humble scripture praying keeps us on track.
2. Teach clearly about ownership in order to establish a clear base of understanding.
3. Remind, review and warn if need be—because church life is constant, and we forget. Be alert in business meetings (II Timothy 4:2).
4. Shepherd, serve, and be an example but never be a lord over God's heritage even when you feel angry (I Peter 5:2-3).
5. Occasionally, as you are led, initiate a public ceremony where everyone agrees in oneness that the church belongs to Jesus.
6. Don't preach for your own glory or use anything about the church for self-advancement. (That's akin to using the Lord's name in vain.)

Let Him lead His own possession.

Reality #13—Relationship– "A Dinner to Enjoy"

Behold, I stand at the door and knock. If anyone hears My voice, and opens the door, I will come in to him and will sup with him, and he with Me. –Revelation 3:20

In his classic book on prayer, O. Hallesbe suggests that the greatest verse on prayer in the Bible is Revelation 3:20. I love this offer from Jesus to dine with us for several reasons. I love the setting—a dinner table. As I reflect on my life, I can safely say that most of my favorite memories took place at some kind of table setting. Secondly, it seems that Jesus **wants** to come into our situation. How much more enjoyable when we know that someone wants to be with us. I note also that it's open-ended. In other words, He will stay as long as we want. Set in the Eastern culture, this is truly a hospitable gesture on Jesus' part.

Can we think about prayer this way? Can we create a culture of prayer that resembles a dinner meeting with Jesus? Did He not open the door for us to open the door for Him? Can we not gather around a table spread with the Bread of His Word? Can we not ask questions of Him and wait for an answer? Can we bless Him with thanks in each other's presence? Are we allowed to stir up thoughts and sharpen one another as we interact in conversational prayer? Absolutely!

This is actually the biblical way for our churches to develop an intimacy with their Lead Pastor as a group. This is praying at its best! This approach is much more enjoyable and effective than the average prayer meeting which shatters hope with long speaking followed by long uncertain times of silence or worrying out loud over mostly outer man needs and constant

"I love to say that life's ultimate privilege is Jesus at my table."

repetition. We can do better than this. We can pray together and nurture this relationship with Jesus.

We who lead God's flock must give thought as to how we can nurture them in this setting. As parents, my wife and I worked hard at making our mealtimes meaningful for the children. We can do the same for our local church.

Down through the years, we have had many very resourceful servants of God at our dinner table. They helped us raise our children. Hearing the life stories of these faithful servants helped anchor our souls in the Kingdom. One time I arranged a lunch with one of my mentors. For four hours, we talked. I loved it. We had evangelists, revivalists, veteran missionaries, and Bible teachers fellowship with us and then graciously pray over us. Just for them to grace us with their presence has made such a difference. How much more, if the guest was Jesus? I love to say that **life's ultimate privilege is Jesus at my table**. Guess what? He wants to be there. So, with Jesus present we can have at our meetings:

1. God's Holy character—where revival begins.
2. God's omnisciently accurate evaluation of our family or church condition.
3. God's all wise solutions.
4. God's promised blessing and reward.

I might add—all free just for opening the door.

"We need to make sure our praying takes us all the way to Jesus."

Let's make a final observation from this letter to the Laodicean church. (Revelation 3:14-21) As I studied this letter in the context of the actual landscape of today's church, I can identify four distinct groups which represent four attitudes of prayer.

The first group prays without heart. These are "rich, increased with goods and have need of nothing" (17a). They think they have no need, so they pray without heart. They are self-centered and self-sufficient.

Group two prays without hope. This group embraces their identity from Jesus as "wretched, and miserable, and poor, and blind, and naked" (v. 17b) and they get stuck there, seemingly unable to move on. They are overwhelmed with need, so they pray without hope. They are problem-centered. The pride of self-pity is seldom recognized. Its chains are strong and deceitful.

Then there are those who pray without rest. These zealots get their fire from Jesus' words in verse 19, "As many as I love, I rebuke and chasten; be zealous therefore, and repent." So, they launch, with all good intention, to take back the kingdom of their own hearts by force. They pray without rest because they are works-centered. All of these so far, I call "subtle substitutes" for Jesus.

The fourth group hears the knock, opens the door, and feast on Jesus' presence. They are true worshippers. They pray with heart, and hope, and rest because they are Christ-centered. This is the place where individuals, families, and churches thrive with love, joy, peace and lasting fruit.

We need to make sure our praying takes us all the way to Jesus.

From Belief to Behavior:

1. Remind your church of the "knock"—He wants to be with us.
2. Remind them of the "table"—This is a dialogue with Him as a group.
3. Use Scripture to form sentence prayers.
4. Suggest that no one pray too long, but everyone pray as many times as led.
5. Reflect on prayer time before leaving. "That was a delightful supper with Jesus."
6. Go rejoicing.

Reality #14—Oneness– The Place to Live

*Neither pray I for these alone, but for them also which shall believe
on me through their word: That they all may be one as thou, Father,
art in me, and I in thee, that they also may be one in us; that the
world may believe that thou hast sent me. And the glory which
thou gavest me I have given them; that they may be one, even as we
are one; I in them, and thou in me, that they may be made perfect
in one and that the world may know that thou hast sent me, and
hast loved them, as thou hast loved me. –John 17:20-23*

Please read the above passage again and again. Immerse
yourself in it until the full power of Jesus' request before the
Father overwhelms every fiber of your being. If Jesus is to be
the lead pastor, then we must surrender our rights to live within
the parameters of His divine request: Oneness, love and glory
must define our attitude within the believing community.

This kind of intentional oneness becomes a witness to the
world that Jesus was sent, that they are loved and that they
may believe. What good does it do to have a sophisticated
mission statement accompanied with energetic outreach
programs if the home base is in pride-driven turmoil?

Paul said it this way: "I therefore, the prisoner of the Lord,
beseech you to walk worthy of the calling with which you were
called, with all lowliness and gentleness, with longsuffering,
bearing with one another in love, endeavoring to keep the
unity of the Spirit in the bond of peace. (Ephesians 4:1-3)
Oneness is both a position we enter into and a practice which
is lived out daily.

On one occasion we had a staff member that always brought a negative spirit to our staff prayer meetings and planning meetings. In my exhaustion with it, I knelt by my chair, claimed my oneness with him in Christ, then asked for the enablement of God's Spirit to respond lovingly to him when we were together. Within a few days the Lord graced him with repentance of a secret sin and oneness was restored.

"We may not always agree on everything, but we can be in oneness about the main thing."

Jesus died and rose again for our oneness and it is delightful. David poetically described it like this.

> *Behold, how good and how pleasant it is*
> *For brethren to dwell together in unity!*
> *It is like the precious oil upon the head,*
> *Running down on the beard, the beard of Aaron,*
> *Running down on the edge of his garments.*
> *   It is like the dew of Hermon,*
> *Descending upon the mountains of Zion;*
> *For there the LORD commanded the blessing—*
> *Life forevermore.*
> Psalms 133:1-3 NKJV

When we work on Oneness in the Spirit of Jesus' prayer, it is fragrant, refreshing and fruitful. A people who live like this will live in a place of blessing.

If this is how Jesus prayed, then certainly this is how He would lead. And if we follow Him, there we will be in a place where we can hear from the Spirit (Revelation 2,3).

From Belief to Behavior:

An under shepherd who is abiding in the Vine (I call these "branch leaders"), regularly reminds the flock of Jesus' request for Oneness and then nurtures them to pray together in accord with Scripture and in the mind of Christ (Philippians 2:5). We may not always agree on everything, but we can be in oneness about the main thing.

Reality #15—Love– The Heart of the Matter

So when they had dined, Jesus saith to Simon Peter, Simon, son of Jonas, lovest thou me more than these? He saith unto him, Yea Lord; thou knowest that I love thee. He saith unto him, Feed my lambs. He saith to him again the second time, Simon, son of Jonas, lovest thou me? He saith unto him, Yea, Lord, thou knowest that I love thee. He saith unto him, Feed my sheep. He saith unto him the third time, Simon, son of Jonas, lovest thou me? Peter was grieved because he said unto him the third time, lovest thou me? And he said unto him, Lord, thou knowest all things: thou knowest that I love thee. Jesus saith unto him, Feed my sheep.
–John 21:15-17

Few scenes in the Bible touch my heart like this one where we find Jesus with breakfast ready for some hungry, tired, confused and fishless fisherman. How like Jesus to be this way. As Lead Pastor He knows when to show up with His love.

He knows just the right questions to ask. "Children, have you any food?" Of course, He knew, but He wanted them to be honest and admit their fishlessness. His questions are often piercing, but His terms are endearing—"children" He calls them.

He knows just the right directions to give. "Cast the net on the right side of the boat and you will find fish." They did and they did. In a short while these "would be" shepherds were around the breakfast fire with 153 fish nearby.

Perhaps Peter was just about dried off when Jesus asked a qualifying question, "Simon, son of Jonah, do you love me

"The gospel record makes it clear that Jesus lived and led out of a heart of love."

more than these?" This question, which was repeated in essence two more times, did two things. First of all, it set the record straight for Peter that he was not a superstar disciple. He could fail with the best of them. Secondly, it identified the heart priority for a proper under-shepherd, "Do you love Me?" Love is the heart of the matter for both the shepherd and the sheep. Feeding, leading, and tending sheep springs from a heart of love for the shepherd and His blood bought purchase. Notice that following Peter's cautious "yes" Jesus' instructions were to "Feed My sheep—My sheep."

The gospel record makes it clear that Jesus lived and led out of a heart of love. Love for the Father love for Jerusalem, love for the multitudes, love for the children, love for God's house (John 2:17) and love for His disciples was the driver behind all that He did—even when He cleansed the temple.

Love should define our ministries. Everything from public preaching to private praying should bubble from a fresh spring of love. We talk to and about Jesus because we love Jesus.

I am thankful that God's love language is obedience. "If you love Me, keep My commandments" (John 14:15) There are times when our hearts may not "feel" anything but during those emotionally dry days we can take the next right step and trust the Lord to bring back the springtime.

The Ephesian church was planted by Paul and pastored by Timothy and John. They served, sacrificed and suffered for Christ but forgot love (Revelation 2:1-7). Labor is no substitute for passion. Separation cannot replace adoration. The heart of the matter is love. That's what pleases Christ and that's what refreshes His people.

Follow our Lead Pastor and pray for the flock to be made perfect with His love (I John 4:17-19).

"Love should define our ministries."

From Belief to Behavior:

1. Review Scriptures that reflect on who Jesus is and what He has done.
2. Have seasons of prayer doing nothing but thanking and praising (use short sentences; take turns).
3. Sing to Him as a group.
4. Remind everyone regularly of this love relationship. Duty alone is exhausting.

Lead Pastor

❦ Section 4 ❧

Headship

Lead Pastor

Dear Shepherd,

The difference between headship and Lordship is the attachment factor. While the church readily confesses Jesus as Lord, it frequently engages some sort of ministry without regard to His headship. He then effectively is only a figurehead and not an active head.

Jesus did not work independently of God the Father, but in union with Him. Jesus never initiated anything on His own. He watched the Father, listened to the Father, and obeyed the Father.

Therefore, give all diligence to make sure His Headship is attached to all ministry activity.

Hold fast to the Head

Reality #16—Headship— Our Place of Protection

For in Him dwelleth all the fulness of the Godhead bodily: and ye are complete in Him who is the head of all principality and power. –Colossians 2:9-10

A good under-shepherd will be very careful to keep his flock under the protection of the headship of the Lead Pastor. This comes through prayerful submission to the Word of God. If, in fact, we do not wrestle against flesh and blood, but against principalities, against powers, against the rulers of the darkness of this age, against spiritual hosts of wickedness in the heavenly places (Ephesians 6:12), then we need to eagerly place ourselves under the Head of all principalities and powers.

Power of any kind without authority is dangerous and activity without authority is exhausting and fruitless. Satan

"Power of any kind without authority is dangerous and activity without authority is exhausting and fruitless." loves to busy a church with noble efforts for which Jesus never planned. All the ills that could be listed about church today could be linked back to this one thing: We have gone our busy and well-intentioned ways without the approval and authority of the active headship of Christ. There is always pain, distraction, and mischief in any congregation where the "strong and right" rule. It's much better to be "weak and victorious" as we watch the Lord of Hosts command His armies to protect His flock. Therefore, strategically and intentionally we must lead those in our care to <u>submit</u>: a military term which means to array under for battle.

Martin Luther's classic hymn, *A Mighty Fortress Is Our God*, poetically captures this idea perfectly.

> *Did we in our own strength confide*
> *Our striving would be losing,*
> *Were not the right man on our side,*
> *The man of God's own choosing,*
> *Dost ask who that may be?*
> *Christ Jesus, it is He—*
> *Lord Sabaoth His name,*
> *From age to age the same—*
> *And He must win the battle—*

Our Lead Pastor is a warrior—both in the Old Testament and in Revelation. He goes forth to conquer and fight for God's people. The rage of the prince of darkness is not a threat to Him. Ours is to humbly and patiently align ourself under

Him and wait until we have His permission with no hidden agenda of our own.

From Belief to Behavior:
- Let's humble ourselves under Christ's authority.
- Repent of all known sin.
- Ask for wisdom in faith.
- Wait until the peace of God rules hearts.
- Do all this as a body.

Note: In all of these lessons we are nurturing an attitude which is led by prayer.

Reality #17—Headship—
The Place of Godly Increase

*And not holding the **Head**, from whom all the body by joints and bands having nourishment ministered, and knit together, increaseth with the increase of God.* –Colossians 2:19

Good news shepherds—the growth of our flocks in quality and quantity comes from Jesus as our Head! Here again is Christ the master builder taking the lead that provides pure growth. Throughout my journey as a pastor-teacher, I was always interested in good leadership ideas. Some of those ideas came from the world of business.

On one occasion I was challenged to write down specific goals for our ministry accompanied with a definite time frame in which they were to be accomplished. So, I did that. The goals were noble I thought. They did include numbers and nickels, but they also included qualities of character and Christlikeness. Having written them on a 3x5 card and putting them in a handy place where they could be reviewed, I set out to see them accomplished.

Shortly after that I heard a very godly mentor of mine say to an audience, "I don't set goals because I might reach them and miss God!" Boy was I conflicted! How was I to reconcile these two approaches to successful accomplishment in kingdom work?

Around that time another mentor shared these words, "Jesus Christ obviously present and actively in charge is our paradigm for success." There was my answer! The life of the body (church) flows from the Head (Christ). I must say I have been fascinated in my faith by this thought ever since. Real increase happens when Jesus is present and in charge in the midst of the redeemed community.

"The life of the body (church) flows from the Head (Christ)."

Paul confirms this truth in the following way.

but speaking the truth in love, may grow up in all things into Him who is the head—Christ—from whom the whole body, joined and knit together by what every joint supplies, according to the effective working by which every part does its share, causes growth of the body for edifying of itself in love.
–Ephesians 4:15-16 NKJV

Within these few words we have all we need for church health and growth. The active headship of Christ provides the power for producing mature, equipped believers. The members of the body cannot do this without Him. No amount of Christian education will transform lives without His power. Remember, the Vine (Jesus) told the disciples, "Without Me you can do nothing" (John 15:5). There is no spiritual growth for the body apart from union with the Head. But with Him we can experience all the aspects of growth and increase that come from God.

We should be reminded here that Jesus promised:

1. To build His church (Matthew 16:18).
2. To accompany His disciple makers (Matthew 28:20).
3. To send the Holy Spirit (Luke 24:49).
4. To walk amongst the church (Revelation 1).

He builds as we preach the Word, walk in obedience, pray in oneness, and serve in the power of the Holy Spirit.

From Belief to Behavior:
- Review the truth (together).
- Repent of missteps (together).
- Agree in prayer (together).
- Take note of what He does (together).
- Rejoice (together).

Reality #18—Headship– The Place of Conflict Resolution

For where two or three are gathered together in My Name, I am there is the midst of them. –Matthew 18:20

The context of this scripture is that of conflict resolution. Jesus is teaching the way of reconciliation for those who are offended (Matthew 18:15-20).

Here again we see Jesus, our Lead Pastor, graciously promising to be present in this process because He knows the natural response to His presence is humility.

My biggest fear in ministry over the years has been that the sheep will begin to fight each other, and I will not be able to stop the fighting. There is nothing worse than to be preaching your heart out, all the while knowing that there is an undercurrent of division in the congregation that snuffs out the fire of every word you say. Satan is a divider. He hands everyone their ammunition yet declares himself neutral. He uses distraction, discouragement, and defection. Churches and homes split because they don't agree upon a platform to be used to resolve conflicts. Scripturally, Jesus is that platform.

Someone's Presence Makes a Difference

Whether it's a hand in the cookie jar or driving too fast on the freeway, someone's presence makes a difference. The sight of a state trooper parked just over the hill can cause a speeding motorist to slow down immediately. One time some families were complaining to me about what was going on in their church. After a moment I asked them, "If the glorified Christ

> *"…He knows the natural response to His presence is humility."*

walked into our midst, what would we do?" Immediately they said, "We would fall on our faces before Him." Great men like Isaiah, Ezekiel and Daniel crumbled in the presence of the glory of God. In the presence of God, attitudes change from "What's wrong with them?" to "Woe is me."

In Revelation 1:12, the beloved Apostle John turned to see who was speaking to him and when he saw Him (v. 17) he said, "I fell at His feet as dead." This dear disciple that leaned on Jesus' breast at the Last Supper could not stand in the presence of His majesty. The practiced presence of Jesus cleanses and humbles every proud worshiper. I might add it also comforts. Jesus then touched John with His right hand and reminded him of whom He was (v. 17-18). What a scene!

Here is a model for our attitude in prayer as we meet to settle our offenses. With all parties in agreement:

1. Let us welcome His presence. (This is a practiced presence.)
2. Let us ask Him to take charge.
3. Let us ask Him to change each individual. (There is often a rub here because most of the time we blame others, but we must be 100% responsible for whatever percent we are wrong even if it is a small percentage.)
4. Let us ask Him to bring us into harmony with the Father and with each other.

I have used this format many times and watched God melt the pride of strong men and women and renew the oneness they had forgotten they had in Christ.

My hobby is playing the piano. I play mostly hymns and simple songs I learned as a young Christian. But I especially enjoy playing when the piano is in tune. To me it's discouraging to try to produce pretty music from an untuned piano. If a tuner comes to bring the instrument up to pitch, he must tune all 88 keys to one standard tuning fork. When he does, a musician is able to then bring forth beautiful harmonies with rich chords.

So it is with the church. When each member is changed in the presence of Jesus and brought into harmony with the Father, a rich song breaks forth for the glory of God and for a witness to the world.

From Belief to Behavior:
- Thank the Lord for His instructions in conflict resolution.
- Thank Him for His promised presence in the same.
- Pray over each conflict in your ministry (as a group when appropriate).
- Commit to the Loyal Covenant of Love.

> *When I survey the wondrous cross*
> *On which the Prince of glory died*
> *My richest gain I count but lost*
> *And pour contempt on all my pride.*

OUR COVENANT OF LOYAL LOVE

We agree to five steps that bind us together with the Father and the Son in the unity of love.

First, we will seek the presence of the Lord Jesus Christ.

We ask His presence in this special relationship of love. We delight in Him and we want Him to delight in us. Our love for Him is our supreme passion.

Second, we will ask Him to take charge of us.

This means that we present our bodies to Him as a living sacrifice to be transformed by the renewing of our mind. We are soldiers reporting to our commander in chief to take charge of us and give us our assignment.

Third, we will ask Him to change each one of us as He sees fit.

We all need to repent again and again until at last Christ presents us faultless before the presence of God's glory with exceeding joy (Jude 24).

Fourth, we will trust Him to bring us into harmony with our Father in heaven.

Jesus prayed that we would share His own unity of love with His Father. It is the duty of all believers to share this unity of love with the Father and the Son. Jesus said that this unity of love is essential for our witness to the world (John 13:34-35; 17:20-23)

Fifth, keeping these four principles prepares us to pray in the power of Jesus' name (John 14:12-14)

We trust God to empower us to keep this unity of love no matter what the cost. If we are deadlocked in conflict, we will seek the help of a mature believer we have chosen. If this fails, we will submit to the leaders of our church to guide us in restoring our unity using the principles taught in Matthew 18:11-35.

Our names and the name of our chosen helper are listed below:

_____   _____

_____   _____

Date: _____

Reality #19—Headship–The Place of Christlike Transformation

But we all, with open face beholding as in a glass the glory of the Lord, are changed into the same image from glory to glory, even as by the Spirit of the Lord. –II Corinthians 3:18

Among the very top ways to recognize Jesus as our lead pastor and master church builder is to pray scripture together. Of course, a shepherd from within the flock needs to facilitate this meeting in a simple way. When we practice scripture praying with humble repentant hearts, the Holy Spirit is free to transform us into His image.

For those readers who may think I am a hopeless mystic, this part may encourage you. Those who know me know that I love expository preaching that presents a clear message from the interpretation of a scripture in its context. I am not a mystic, but I am trying to understand the mystery of "Christ in us the hope of glory." So, take heart and let me rush to the believer's ultimate privilege in the presence of Jesus.

First of all let me say, prayer will always be boring and powerless if it's only a monologue, i.e., us talking to God. Oh, the dread of my early experience in prayer meetings. After a Bible study, prayer requests, mostly outer man needs, would go on and on. We would break into groups—men with men and women with women. The men would pray around the circle basically repeating all the same requests with varying clichés. They talked and repeated and informed God of all these things that He evidently wasn't aware of—all with our heads bowed and eyes closed! I still don't like it to be that way.

"...the best way to listen to God is through His written Word."

Prayer is meant to be a dialogue where listening to God becomes as much a part as talking to God.

Praying for the strength of the inner man is always better than just praying for the healing of the outer man. "The spirit of a man will sustain his infirmity, but a wounded spirit who can bear" (Proverbs 18:14).

Secondly, the best way to listen to God is through His written Word. We pray best with our Bibles open—and maybe with our eyes open! Why not? Let's say our church is praying about the marriages of our families. Why not open our Bibles to classic passages on marriage and formulate prayers from the verses in front of us? Why not take time in prayer meetings to write prayers on 3x5 cards, then read our freshly crafted thoughts back to God in the hearing of our fellow prayer warriors? It sure beats vain repetition and shallow thoughts off the top of our heads.

I heard one Bible teacher say, "If I pray from my mind, I generally pray for only a few minutes. If I pray from my heart, I can pray longer. If I pray from scripture, I can pray all day." How true. I used to think Bible study and prayer had to be two separate things. For many years now, I have lumped them together, meditating on the text and praying for it to be true of my life and the life of our church. I truly pray best with my Bible open.

Finally, if done right, we will be transformed in the place of prayer. To be like Him is the goal and privilege of our praying. The entrance of God's Word gives light and understanding (Psalms 119:130). Here's a verse I cherish that gives me great hope for my life and our churches, "But we all, with unveiled face beholding as in a mirror the glory of the

Lord, are being transformed into the same image from glory to glory just as by the Spirit of the Lord" (II Corinthians 3:18 NKJV). Warren Wiersbe says it best. "When the child of God looks into the Word of God and sees the Son of God, he is changed into the image of God, by the Spirit of God for the glory of God."

Here's the point. Humbly praying scripture back to the Lord transforms the individual and the church who practices the same. Our wandering hearts are most satisfied when we realize that our metamorphosis results in our life being replaced by His. Beholding our transformation is life's ultimate fulfillment. This is what happens when we pray and humbly engage the scriptures with Christ obviously present and actively in charge. If believers and churches want to change, this is where it starts. Transformation and ongoing revival can be the experience of any church who humbly prays with Bibles open, because our lives are replaced by His.

Those sad and confused disciples on the road to Emmaus (Luke 24) were empowered with burning hearts (v. 32) because Jesus began at Moses and the prophets and explained all the Scriptures concerning Himself. He opened the Scriptures to them. Soon they would join with the others and be used to turn the world upside down (Acts 17:6). This Jesus is the foremost reason for being an intentional part of the prayer life of your church. When He is, we too can see Him with the eye of the Spirit and become transformed by the saving life of Christ. When we know Him, see Him, and are changed by Him, the fullness of joy launches us out from the inside of our hearts to talk about Him.

From Belief to Behavior:

• Prayer fully assesses the needs of the flock (This could follow the passion of the preaching at any given time).

• Present appropriate passages of Scripture which relate to the need and give a brief sense of the meaning.

• In faith and repentance ask the Lord for individual and corporate transformation from the inside out.

• Go rejoicing.

Reality #20—Headship— The Place for Homebuilders

Likewise, ye husbands, dwell with them according to knowledge, giving honour unto the wife, as unto the weaker vessel, and as being heirs together of the grace of life; that your prayers be not hindered. –I Peter 3:7

Do you pray together? A member of a church mission committee asked a couple who were being examined for possible support. After an awkward pause, the husband replied, "We both pray, but we do not pray together." They are not alone. Many Christian couples including pastors and veteran missionaries do not pray together. Nine out of ten Americans say they pray but only about 14% pray together with their family, close friends, or their church.

Practicing the headship of Christ as a community starts at home. Our marriages especially are an outward illustration of the gospel (Ephesians 5:22-23). Nothing I've ever done in ministry has produced more lasting fruit than simply taking my wife by the hand and praying with her to begin our day.

In my experience, the care of the emotional (giving honor), intellectual (with understanding), physical (dwell with them), and spiritual (being heirs together of the grace of life) needs of our wives begins when we take their hand and pray with them. Here again our Lead Pastor has established our priorities starting at home. Public prayers and preaching are severely hindered when there is division at home.

For us as husbands it is easy to get bitter when the love and respect cycle becomes the crazy cycle. We are warned,

> *"Practicing the headship of Christ as a community starts at home."*

"Husbands, love your wives and do not be bitter toward them" (Colossians 3:19). Everyone knows there are times when we must war against our feelings in order to surrender in the holy place.

The main reason we must pray together is to unite under the authority of the Lord Jesus Christ. The Scripture is clear that God is the head of Jesus, Jesus is the head of every man, and the man is the head of the woman (I Corinthians 11:3). Clearly Jesus is the head of our homes and needs to be the "constant consultant" in all of our affairs. God's instruction to Israel about the home was definitive.

Hear, O Israel: The LORD our God, the LORD is one. You shall love the LORD your God with all your heart, with all your soul, and with all your strength.

And these words which I command you today shall be in your heart. You shall teach them diligently to your children and shall talk of them when you sit in your house, when you walk by the way, when you lie down, and when you rise up. –Deuteronomy 6:4-7 NKJV

A successful home starts with a covenant love relationship with God, is regulated by the truth of God's Word, applied to every area of life, and nurtured by meaningful conversations during the natural pauses of home life.

When a couple or family meet for sincere prayer, here's what they are saying:

1. "Lord, we love You and want to be with You."
2. "Lord, we are totally dependent on You for everything."
3. "Lord, we know preeminence belongs to You."
4. "Lord, You are the Head of our home."
5. "Lord, bring us into harmony with You and each other.

Someone said, "Home is the place where life makes up its mind." When parents pray together, kids get the idea and freedom to make prayer the way to live day by day.

From Belief to Behavior:
- Form a habit (time and place).
- Facilitate the habit (tools).
- Keep it simple.
- Make it fun.
- Start upward (Scripture).
- Go inward (heart needs).
- Then outward (hands at work).
- Go rejoicing (hug).

Reality #21—Headship– A Place of Fullness of Joy

And now come I to thee; and these things I speak in the world, that they might have My joy fulfilled in themselves. –I Peter 3:7

When Jesus is our Lead Pastor, we can count on Him being desperately interested in our joy. Having lived in the Godhead with the Father, He has experienced the ultimate joy. In fact, Psalms 16:11 is David speaking prophetically of Christ's resurrection as referenced in Acts 2:28, "You will show me the path of life; In your presence is fullness of joy; At your right hand are pleasures forevermore." This is the way Jesus felt when He was in the Father's presence and this is the way He wants His church to relate in an unbroken fellowship with the Father.

A good balance statement here is to say, "Joy is not the absence of trouble, but rather the presence of the Lord." Joy truly is the serious business of heaven and a church needs to sense that they are being carried by the Lord rather than being driven by man.

Here are some amazing direct quotes from the Bible in Jesus' own words. "These things I have spoken to you, that My joy may remain in you and that your joy may be full" (John 15:11). Jesus made this statement while face to face with His disciples. There was something about His joy that He wanted them to have which was like a "jump start" for their joy. He said something similar in John 17:13, but this time He was in prayer with His heavenly Father. Here it is, "But now I come to you, and these things I speak in the world, that they may have My joy fulfilled in themselves." These are amazing words and they come from <u>His Holiness</u> spoken in the <u>Holy of Holies</u>. For a world that is looking for love and happiness in all the wrong places this should be a warning. But for sad, discouraged, grumpy, and self-pitied Christians, this should give us hope! Jesus cares about our joy and has prayed for it—yes—lived for it and died for it.

"Joy is not the absence of trouble, but rather the presence of the Lord."

Why was Jesus so joyful? Listen to these words spoken from the Father to Jesus and recorded in Hebrews 1:8-9. "But to the Son He says: 'Your throne, O God, is forever and ever; a scepter of righteousness is the scepter of Your kingdom. You have loved righteousness and hated lawlessness; therefore God, Your God, has anointed You with the oil of gladness more than your companions.'" I love those words "oil of gladness". Because Jesus loved righteousness and hated lawlessness and lived in unbroken fellowship with His Father, He was anointed with supreme gladness.

Most churches want to be and need to be missional, intentional, and strategic. What joy it should bring to our congregation when they learn that the Father has given Jesus, our Lead Pastor, the nations, "Ask of Me, and I will give You the nations for Your inheritance and the ends of the earth for Your possession." (Psalms 2:8 NKJV) It is already the Father's heart for all nations to *Kiss the Son* (Psalms 2:12). He also offers a blessing on all who put their trust in Him (Psalms 2:12b). These prophetic words were given 1000 years before Jesus came in the flesh and will be completely fulfilled at His return. In the meantime, our churches can set their sail and catch the wind of the Father's will for His Son. We are not fighting a losing battle. When we have Jesus in the lead, we are becoming one with the Godhead in the Father's mission. The Kingdom is already but not yet; we are obeying our part of the mission. We are not fighting a losing battle. We are more than conquerors in God's kingdom where God reigns through God's people over God's place, and that should bring us joy. In fact, it is a mini demonstration of a little heaven on earth.

From Belief to Behavior:
- Review the Scriptures used.
- Believe them.
- Pray them up to the Lord.
- Go rejoicing.

Reality #22—Headship– The Way of Ultimate Success

I have glorified thee on the earth. I have finished the work which thou gavest Me to do. –John 17:4

Every pastor I've ever known has at some level wanted to be successful. But success in ministry is often very hard to evaluate. We can look at the size of the crowd or the amount of the offering, the professions of faith or number of baptisms and yet never really know how our ministries are doing. An appearance can sometimes be deceiving. In fact, Jesus said to the church at Ephesus who seemed to have it all together, "You have left your first love" (Revelation 2:4) To the church at Sardis He said, "You have a name that you are alive, but you are dead" (Revelation 3:1). Of course, the church at Laodicea made Jesus sick to His stomach because they thought they were rich and wealthy and had need of nothing. Jesus then said, "You are wretched, miserable, poor, blind, and naked…" (Revelation 3:17). Jesus knows how we really are.

Here again is where our "Lead Pastor" demonstrates the way of true success. He marched to the beat of one drummer— His Father. There is nothing wrong in wanting to be successful as long as it's in the right ways and for the right reasons. Most never think about Jesus and the idea of success going together, but they do. Jesus was perfect in all of His ways, obedient to every detail, and finished everything the Father planned for Him to do. He remains God's immaculate example of success for all of us.

"The key to Jesus' leadership was the relationship He had with His Father."

The key to Jesus' leadership was the relationship He had with His Father. Salvation's plan had always belonged to the Father. Jesus' high priestly prayer is saturated with this idea of watching the Father then moving in obedience. Along with our introductory verse above, we also have these words.

I have manifested Your name to the men whom You have given Me out of the world. –John 17:6 NKJV

Now they have known that all things which you have given Me are from You. For I have given to them the words which You have given Me; ... those whom You gave Me I have kept ... I have given them your word; –John 17:8,14 NKJV

Do you see the pattern? Jesus first developed His relationship with the Father, received all from Him and then ministered the Father's word and will to the people. That was the key to His success and so it is for us if Jesus is to be our active head and Lead Pastor.

Very subtly brainstorming strategy meetings and goal setting in our enthusiasm can cloud the way to the Father. This is not necessarily wrong in itself as long as it doesn't replace or interrupt intimacy with the Godhead on the personal and corporate level. Cultivate the habit with our stewardship to stop and meet with the Father, the Son, and the Holy Spirit in order to get on their agenda.

So how do we know Jesus was a success? Peter's fiery message on the day of Pentecost identifies six reasons why we know Jesus succeeded in His Father's eyes (Acts 2:22-40).

1. God (Father) publicly endorsed Him (v. 22).
2. God released Him from the horrors of death (2v. 4a).
3. God raised Him back to life (v. 24b; v. 32).
4. God exalted Him to the place of highest honor (In heaven)—His right hand (v. 33a; Hebrews 8:1, 10:12).
5. God gave Him the Holy Spirit (v. 33b) to administer.
6. God made Him Lord and Christ (Messiah) (v. 36).

Now "Christ who has gone into heaven, is at the right hand of God, and all the angels, authorities and powers accept His authority" (I Peter 3:22).

May our ministries also receive the endorsement of the Father and stand against all evil because we followed His lead at all cost.

From Belief to Behavior:
- Have regular stops for accountability in activity.
- Pray scripture over everything together.
- Don't move until you are told.
- Rejoice.

Reality #23—Headship–
A Friend in Lament

Now from the sixth hour there was darkness over all the land unto the ninth hour. And about the ninth hour Jesus cried with a loud voice, saying, "Eli, Eli, lama sabachthani?" that is to say, "My God, My God, why hast thou forsaken Me?" –John 17:4

A healthy church must learn how to lament well together, and no one understands like Jesus about lament. At the cross it was as though all of creation was identifying with the Creator. Three days of darkness occurred in Egypt before Passover (Exodus 10:21-23) and three hours of darkness covered the land before the Lamb of God died for the sins of the world.

Because we live in a sin cursed world, very often a part of our church body will be called into painful moments and we need to follow our Lead Pastor, Jesus, into His perfect ability to weep with those who weep. He knows just how to stop and look with undivided attention, listen to every heart, touch every need and cry out with those who seem to have no answer at the moment.

In his very excellent book, *Dark Clouds, Deep Mercy, Discovering the Grace of Lament,* Mark Vroegop defined lament as a **"prayer in pain that leads to trust."** He says, "Lament is how we live between the poles of a hard life and trusting in God's sovereignty. Christianity suffers when lament is missing. …to pray in pain, even with its messy struggle and tough questions, is an act of faith where we open up our hearts to God."[9]

Sadly, under my leadership, the counsel for difficult times has often fallen under two

"Christianity suffers when lament is missing."

categories: Either "Be still and know that I am God" or "Victory in Jesus." I am learning, but have not taught or modeled well, the grace of lament. Vroegop says, "To cry is human but to lament is Christian." He calls it—worship in the minor key.

There is one who models lament perfectly. Whether He was seeing the multitudes, overlooking the city of Jerusalem, or dying on the cross, He knew how to process His perfect life of obedience through times of lament. When we operate under His active headship, He can infuse an entire congregation with His Holy Spirit who knows how to grieve perfectly.

Sometimes trials are not overcome quickly. A process is often needed in order to allow individuals to steward their pain yet grow in trust and in faith. Meeting with Jesus obviously present and actively in charge lays the foundation and establishes the true Spirit of lament on behalf of those who are in the Refiners fire. How good it is to be surrounded by a body of believers, who by the power and words of Jesus cry and believe with us. There is one, and one only, to whom God listens and always listens; He is Jesus. Standing at the tomb of Lazarus Jesus prayed, "Father, I thank You that You have heard Me. And I know that you always hear Me" (John 11:41-42). That same One authored the Psalms and sang the Psalms of which one third are songs of lament.

Dietrich Bonhoeffer said it well, "In Jesus' mouth the human word becomes God's Word. When we pray along with the prayer of Christ, God's Word becomes again a human word. Thus, all prayers of the Bible are such prayers which we pray together with Jesus Christ, prayers in which Christ includes us,

"No one understands like Jesus."

and through which Christ brings us before the face of God. Otherwise there are no true prayers, for only in and with Jesus Christ can we truly pray"(From *Teaching Psalms*, Vol. 1 by Christopher Ash).

Praying together in Jesus's Name (John 14:14) is often applied to something we want to accomplish or acquire but seldom is our authority in prayer focused on the process of lament during a time of pain with others. Through an understanding of the heart and ability of our Lead Pastor Jesus and guided by the content in the Psalms of lament, we can minister with power to those in our church as they are being transformed into the image of Christ through trials.

No one understands like Jesus. No one ever cared for us like Jesus. And no one every prays for us like Jesus (John 17, Hebrews 2:17,18; 4:14,15; 7:25).

From Belief to Behavior:
Review the priesthood of Jesus.
Review the Psalms of lament.
Rehearse the process of lament together (Vroegop).

1. Keep turning to prayer.
2. Bring your complaints.
3. Ask boldly.
4. Choose to trust.

☙ Section 4 ❧

The Stewardship
of Grace

Lead Pastor

Dear Shepherd,

The heart desire of God is to bestow great grace on the church through Jesus Christ and thus gain great glory in the church by Jesus Christ.

He gives grace for boldness, for giving, for suffering, etc. according to His way of getting glory through a particular church in its context.

Observing His grace bestowed and responding to it allows us to steward well the gifts given. These stewardships actually determine the ministry functions of our church and allow our people to minister by grace and not by grudge.

Give all diligence to observe where God is working in your church, point it out to the sheep, then respond accordingly.

Great grace was upon them all

Reality #24—The Stewardship of Grace

… Paul and Barnabas: Who speaking to them, persuaded them to continue in the grace of God. –Acts 13:43

The life and authority of Christ invades the church through divinely orchestrated acts of grace.

<u>Our Stewardship</u>: To observe carefully and cherish what God initiates. Jesus is always in the lead if we will take time to notice His footprints of grace.

God, by grace, is the initiator of all Kingdom activity. Our effectiveness in ministry comes as we learn to observe His activity, cherish what He is doing and cooperate. Here's what Jesus the Vine says to us, "Ye have not chosen Me, but

> *"God, by grace, is the initiator of all Kingdom activity."*

I have chosen you and ordained you that ye should go and bring forth fruit, and that your fruit should remain: that whatsoever ye shall ask of the Father in My name, He may give it you" (John 15:16).

My ministry mindset immediately began to change the first time I heard Manley Beasley say, "Jesus never initiated anything but rather waited on His Father." Jesus Himself said, My Father worked hitherto, and I work" (John 5:17). Again, He reinforced, "Verily, verily I say unto you, the Son can do nothing of Himself, but what He seeth the Father do: for what things so ever He doeth, these also doeth the Son likewise" (John 5:19). Jesus said, "I can of mine own self do nothing: as I hear, I judge: and My judgment is just, because I seek not Mine own will but the will of the Father which hath sent Me" (John 5:30).

Jesus is telling us that He obeyed the Father's will, did the Father's work, and spoke the Father's words. God alone initiates anything that is eternal. "We love Him because He first loved us" (I John 4:19). History is always His-story. He chose to create, His grace found Noah, called Abraham and Moses and raised up the judges and the prophets. He ordained John the Baptist, sent Jesus through the Virgin, called Peter for the Jews and Paul for the Gentiles. He gave the Revelation of Jesus to Jesus and signified it by His angel unto His servant John (Revelation 1:1). So why, for years, did I think that I had to come up with genius ideas to sell them to my congregation, then whip them into action and make something happen for God? Because that was all I knew from the impressions I was given. Well-meaning, I was missing God's movement of grace.

To the church, Jesus has been given to be the active Head of all things (Ephesians 1:22). He is the Groom who initiates and we the church are the bride who responds to Him as our Beloved. So the life of the Vine—Jesus—enters the soul of the church by grace and we are blessed.

Grace brings salvation (Titus 2:11), teaches us to live godly (Titus 2:12, 13), to give generously (2 Corinthians 9:6), enables us to suffer joyfully (2 Corinthians 12:9), and serve acceptably (Hebrews 12:28). This is none other than the dynamic life of Christ in the soul of the church giving her the desire and power to obey God. I love Acts 4:33, which capsulizes the church condition. "And with great power the apostles gave witness of the resurrection of the Lord Jesus; and great grace was upon them all." (NKJV)

So, where do church servants look for grace?

1. In every person who walks through the door. Where are they in their faith journey and how can the church serve them in taking the next step of faith? No respecter of persons, please, and don't forget the babies.
2. In open door opportunities. Be wise to distractions but alert to relationships.
3. Through heart changes. Testimonies from changed hearts can crosspollinate spiritual growth in others and build a platform for ministry.
4. Through heart stirrings. God is in the business of calling out men like Paul and Barnabas to His work.
5. Through repentance and faith in salvation. Celebrations over the newly born-again bring joy and encouragement. Make a big deal of the attitude of repentance.

6. Through natural and supernatural giftedness. Do a survey of gifts, passions, and callings. Give each person a place to use them. Empower and resource them for their ministry.

7. Through knowledge. Do your best to tap the intelligence of your congregation and show respect for their knowledge. Don't be afraid of the smart ones and don't belittle those who seem limited. Still water often runs deep, and everyone knows something you don't.

8. Physical resources. Every church has resources available to them. We are more wealthy than we realize. The key is recognizing them as gifts from God to be employed in spreading the gospel. Don't "poor mouth" your congregation. Give them respect and dignity for who they are and what they have. Say "grace" over them.

9. Don't forget hardships. It is clear that God uses trials to build bridges which lead to relationships and ministry. Grief share is a magnet for ministry. People admire your strengths, but they really relate to your weakness.

10. Other ministries—Don't be an island to yourself. No ministry is a know all, do all, self-sufficient fortress. We need to network, share resources and partner with others who can bring to the table things we need but don't have. This helps the function of ministry and the attitude we reflect.

The list above is meant to get you started in looking for grace. There are many more. Just keep looking.

Let me finish this reality with three short yet important reminders.

1. We can be steadfast and diligent while we are watching.

After the great movement of God's grace initiative at Pentecost where three thousand souls were saved, the church activity was described like this, "And they continued steadfastly in the apostle's doctrine and fellowship, and in breaking of bread, and in prayers" (Acts 2:42).

Since the Day of Pentecost, the four functioning operatives of the church have remained the same.

1. Scripture examination
2. Accountable fellowship
3. Gospel review and remembrance
4. Prayer connection with Jesus

Evangelism was a natural by-product which grew out of this transforming fellowship. The point here is that, while we function by grace, who don't have to be "graced out" doing nothing while waiting on grace. God has clearly outlined our function and we can continue steadfastly in season and out of season.

One time I attended a revival conference where the speaker was clearly emphasizing sovereign visitation of grace as in Jonathan Edward's revivals. During an interactive time one person asked, "What do we do in the meantime while we wait for such visitations?" The answer given has encouraged me through many dry seasons, "Be busy about the biblical disciplines of the church and preach the Word." That is sound advice that always stands the test of time and weathers any storm.

2. Cherish and treasure every morsel of grace made available by God no matter how small it seems. The Lord loves it when we really value His gifts. God loves a cheerful giver, but He also loves a thankful receiver. When talking about the Word of God, here's what Jesus said, "For whosoever hath, to him shall be given, and he shall have more abundance; but whosoever hath not, from him shall be taken away even that he hath" (Matthew 13:12). He gives this same truth in the parable of the talents (Matthew 25:29).

What does this mean to us who are seeking to be good stewards of God's grace initiatives in our lives? In the words of Matthew Henry, "There are those to whom this knowledge is not given, and a man can receive nothing unless it is given him from above (John 3:27) and be it remembered that God is debtor to no man; his grace is his own; he gives or withholds it as pleasure (Romans 11:35). The difference must be resolved into God's sovereignty. Note the rule God observes in dispensing His gifts. He bestows them on those who improve them but takes them away from those who bury them. Here is a promise to him that has true grace and uses what he has is promised more abundance.

Speak often of the grace God has given to your congregation. Help them see it, too. Celebrate God's gifts and invest them in Kingdom ministry. The motivational gifts in Romans 12:3-8 have been very helpful to me as I have sought to match gifts with ministry.

A few years ago, this idea of stewarding the grace you have was illustrated on a mission trip my wife and I took to Nicaragua. Our daughter Johanna and her husband Bob were ministering there, equipping Latino pastors for their work. One day Bob and I visited one of the pastors who shepherded the flock who literally lived in the city dump. This was a congregation that lived resourcefully from what the city of Managua threw away, yet the pastor of

"Humility is the starting point for Life with God."

the "Lathureka" trash heap found grace to have purpose and vision for his sheep. Grace always wins the day.

3. <u>Never forget that humility always precedes grace</u> in the lives of believers. A proud church will find itself fighting against the Lord Himself, "God resists the proud but gives grace to the humble" (James 4:6). A church that continues well in the stewardship of grace must be vigilant about taking spiritual inventory starting with the leadership. No matter how well we may appear to be doing, we can still be failing because we have left the sense of our desperation for Jesus in a first-love relationship like the Ephesian church in Revelation 2. We can be deceived into thinking that we are rich and increased with goods and have need of nothing like the Laodocean church in Revelation. Such an attitude can overtake us in our lack of awareness and make Jesus want to vomit, as you well know (Revelation 3:16). In the words of Del Fehsenfeld III, "Humility is the starting point for Life with God" (*Revive Magazine*, August 2015).

From Belief to Behavior:
   Have a gathering to:
      1. Bow low before the Lord.
      2. Point out all forms of Grace evident in your ministry.
      3. Ask for wisdom in how to move forward in cooperation with what God has initiated.

Reality #25—The Stewardship of Faith

For unto us was the gospel preached, as well as unto them; but the word preached did not profit them, not being mixed with faith in them that heard it. –Hebrews 4:2

The life and authority of Christ is embraced by definite acts of faith (The Stewardship of Faith).

<u>Our Stewardship:</u> To mix faith with everything—the good, the bad and the ugly.

We must never stop applying scripture truth to any situation and we must never drop the shield of faith, "The first and primary work of the church is faith in Jesus Christ." The first time I heard Ian Murray say that, it stopped me in my tracks because that's not what I had been taught. My thinking was more along the lines of evangelism, discipleship or Bible instruction. So, I shelved the idea for a while until I realized that faith in Christ's movements of grace was the birthplace of ministry functions (Galatians 5:6).

The heroes of the faith moved in faith to God's promptings of grace and moved the gospel story along during their watch. Abel offered a more excellent sacrifice by faith; Enoch was translated by faith because of his grace to please God. Noah prepared an ark by faith because of God's grace in a warning of things not yet seen. His faith even had some fear in it. Abraham left home by faith because of the grace of God's call. He wasn't sure where he was going but he was about to see, with the eye of faith, a better city with a greater builder than anything he knew in Ur of Chaldees (Hebrews 11:1-10). You know the list goes on. Remember, the idea here is for us to steward the movements of God's grace by embracing them by faith and being scripturally obedient in

"... faith in Christ's movements of grace was the birthplace of ministry functions."

every one of them. The story God is writing in and through your church may appear like a mountain path that makes many "hair pin" turns while approaching the summit which, by the way, you may never see before the end of your watch. Once again, I cite our heroes, "These all died in faith *not* having received the promises, but having seen them afar off, and were persuaded of them and embraced them, and confessed that they were strangers and pilgrims on the earth (Hebrews 11:13). Yours may only be to see afar off but believing and obeying is yours for today. In fact, God makes it clear when he says, "But without faith it is impossible to please Him, for he that cometh to God must believe that He is and that He is a rewarder of those who diligently seek Him" (Hebrews 11:6). A ministry that turns every movement and challenge into a treasure hunt for God will experience God's reward. God has great plans in mind for a people who will call and pray and seek and search for Him with all their hearts (Jeremiah 29:11-13).

Sometimes our ministries do not appear to be doing that well. In fact, they may seem to be stalled or going backward—even after we have identified clear promises and directions of God's moving by grace. During these times it's really easy to second guess ourselves or slump in bewilderment over what God is doing or not doing. The prophet Habakkuk helps us out during these "death-valley" days. His book starts with a bitter lament over Israel's condition. Godly King Josiah's reforms have been quickly overturned by his successor Jehoiakim, and

"A ministry that turns every movement and challenge into a treasure hunt for God will experience God's reward."

Habakkuk has some serious questions; "O Lord, how long shall I cry, and thou wilt not hear? Why dost thou shew me iniquity and cause me to behold grievance? —the law is slacked and judgment doth never go forth; for the wicked doth compass about the righteous; therefore, wrong judgment proceedeth" (1:2-4). Allow me to paraphrase, "Why, God, are You letting things go so long and get so bad without doing anything?" God answers, "Behold—I will work a work in your days, which ye will not believe, though it be told you—. I will raise up the Chaldeans, that bitter and hasty nation, which shall march through the breadth of the land, to possess the dwelling places that are not theirs. They are terrible and dreadful; —they shall come all for violence—he shall passover, and offend, imputing this his power unto his god" (1:5-11). Basically, God answered Habakkuk's question with, "I am going to do something. My plan is already in place and on the way. I am going to bring an evil army across the nation that will loot and kill and destroy. He will then add insult to injury by setting up idols and worship centers to his false god and give him the credit." This answer so stunned the prophet that he got very quiet and cautious and said, "I will stand upon my watch, and set me upon the tower, and will watch to see what he will say unto me, and what I shall answer when I am reproved" (2:1). He did the right thing. His questioning turned to listening. His pacing turned to standing still. His way forward was to stop. **Sometimes the best movement of faith is to not move at all and yet believe in the character of God.** One time I was invited to take over a very troubled ministry. After a short assessment, I told the leadership.

"We must call this ministry to a complete stop." Basically, I was giving them permission to rest from striving and trying to make things happen.

"When God can't be understood, He can be embraced by faith and that makes Him very happy."

Back to our friend Habakkuk—Patrick Morley says it best, "There was the God that Habakkuk wanted and there was the God that was, and they were not the same." Often in our ministries, God doesn't seem to behave as we would like. Our call is still to believe. In fact, if I could condense this chapter into one sentence, it would be this; When God can't be understood, He can be embraced by faith and that makes Him very happy. Habakkuk's name means "one who embraces." At times we must do the same.

The healthy dialogue between the prophet and God yielded three answers from God that provide pillars for the faith of any believing servant of God during any conditions.

1. "—The just shall live by his faith" (2:4). This signature verse repeated three times in the New Testament lets us know that, if we are going to live with God, we are going to live by faith.
2. "—The earth shall be filled with the knowledge of the glory of the Lord, as the waters cover the sea (2:14). Someday everybody will get it, and it doesn't all have to happen today or through us.
3. "—The Lord is in His holy temple; let all the earth keep silence before Him" (2:20), In other words, "Be still, and know that I am God; I will be exalted in the earth. The Lord of hosts is with us; the God of Jacob is our refuge. Selah" (Psalm 46:10, 11).

God knows we are in ministry, and He is as pleased with our believing hearts as He is with our working hands. You may have to say to some of the anxious folks around, "This is a time for us to stand still, be still and listen." Then give permission to only believe.

Through this experience, Habakkuk came out with a new song—one written from a real-life experience. Here are the lyrics.

Habakkuk's Song

Although the fig tree shall not blossom,
Neither shall fruit be in the vines;
The labour of the olive shall fail,
And the fields shall yield no meat;
The flock shall be cut off from the fold,
And there shall be no herd in the stalls;
Yet I will rejoice in the Lord of my salvation.
The Lord God is my strength,
And He will make my feet, like hindsfeet,
And He will make me walk upon
Mine high places.
(Habakkuk 3:17-19)

So, after some great movements of grace when expectations soar, don't be surprised if the landscape looks bleak. Remember, if God can't be understood, He can be embraced by faith. And if you will lay down any pride and believe the best is yet to come because the Lord is in His holy temple, you too may sing a new song and tell a new story of faith which only brings more grace.

Finally, Jesus Himself gives us instruction to let faith in Him be our first and primary work. In John 6, we find

Jesus being pursued by the multitudes. He knew they were only "bread and fish" followers and told them so

"Jesus considers our faith in Him to be our greatest calling and priority work."

when He said, "Ye seek Me, not because ye saw the miracles, but because ye did eat of the loaves, and were filled." He then challenged their values by saying, "Labour not for the meat which perisheth, but for that meat which endureth unto everlasting life—" (v. 27). They responded with this question, "What shall we do, that we might work the work of God?" (v. 28) Jesus answered, "This is the work of God, that ye believe on Him whom He hath sent" (v. 29).

Jesus considers our faith in Him to be our greatest calling and priority work. Everything flows from that. He loves it when we really believe that what we believe is really real. In ministry, if we are going to live with God, we are going to live by faith. Paul said, "For in Jesus Christ neither circumcision availeth anything nor uncircumcision but faith which works by love" (Galatians 5:6). When the stewardship of faith becomes the lifestyle of our church, there will be a growing core of believers who discover Him to not only be their salvation but also their sufficiency and satisfaction.

From Belief to Behavior:
1. Review how the heroes of the faith embraced their call of grace.
2. List your present circumstances as a church which must be embraced even though not understood.
3. Thank the Lord for the trial of your faith.
4. Believe God together in prayer verbalizing your trust.
5. Pray for wisdom.

Reality #26—The Stewardship of Worship

… Worthy is the Lamb that was slain to receive power, and riches, and wisdom, and strength, and honour, and glory, and blessing,

… Blessing and honour, and glory, and power, be unto Him that sitteth upon the Throne, and unto the Lamb for ever and eve.
–Hebrews 4:2

The life and authority of Christ continues by regular acts of worship (The Stewardship of Worship).

Our Stewardship: To maintain a first love relationship with Jesus through scripture-based adoration.

Action: Constantly remind the flock that worship is a lifestyle where we do all things for an audience of ONE. This simple yet powerful approach was perfectly modeled by Jesus Himself.

This reality is only meant to discuss the subject of worship as it relates to the church's first love relationship with Jesus. All churches begin to lose the power of grace through faith when they leave their first love. A reviving brings new life, new life leads to new ministries, new ministries lead to new busy schedules, new initiatives, new ideas, new standards and with good intent we "leave town without Jesus." He gets lost because of "the company" (Luke 2:44). The reality of church life is that we will always find ourselves fighting for first love. Our ministries will not drift into first love. Even a "purpose-driven" church must be very careful to assure that love for Jesus drives our intentions.

Sometimes our ambition can become our worst enemy, especially if the Lord graces us with bountiful resources.

The Ephesian church had enjoyed great grace from God. The apostle Paul, along with Timothy and the apostle John, had started the church at Ephesus. Paul was greatly loved by the church there. When he was about to leave after reporting to them for the last time, they hugged him and kissed him and cried because he said he would never see them again (Acts 20:36-38).

The Lord Jesus, the Head of the church, our Lead Pastor, gives His assessment of this great church.

I know thy works, and thy labour, and thy patience, and how thou canst not bear them which are evil; and thou hast tried them which say they are apostles, and are not and hast found them liars; and hast borne, and hast patience, and for my Name's sake hast labored, and hast not fainted. –Revelation 2:2, 3

These were a suffering people who were patient, hated evil, tried false apostles, persevered, worked hard without quitting for Jesus's name. From the outside, they looked almost perfect. But Jesus knew their hearts were growing cold toward Him and described them as having left their first love. Something we need to remember here is that when our love for Jesus grows cool, so does our love for each other. If we are honest, we have to admit that Jesus is easier to love than people. Often we fail to recognize that the compromised ministry and outreach of our church started with our interrupted love for Jesus.

Jesus, with His omnisciently accurate assessment, faithfully reveals to the Ephesian church their problems, then tells them what to do about it.

Nevertheless I have somewhat against thee, because thou hast left thy first love. Remember therefore from whence thou art fallen, and repent, and do the first works; or else I will come unto thee quickly, and will remove thy candlestick out of his place, except thou repent. –Revelation 2:4, 5

He gives them a divinely solemn ultimatum. They could remember, repent, and return their hearts to Him, or He would remove their candlestick! That's scary! While we might excuse a cold heart for Jesus as an "acceptable sin," He sees it as a reason to close a church down!

Here are some general observations.

1. A church can appear to be doing everything right and still be in trouble.
2. Leaving our first love is a sin and grieves Jesus.
3. Leaving our first love can lead to the removal of our witness as a church.
4. We can listen and change and be blessed.
   He that hath an ear let him hear what the Spirit saith unto the churches; to Him that overcometh will I give to eat of the tree of life, which is in the midst of the paradise of God (Revelation 2:7).
5. The Lord Himself knows all the intimate details. This should always be a great comfort to any leader. It should also be a call to prayer.

This raises two major questions in my mind. What is first love, and what are first works?

Anything I've ever read or heard on the subject of first love related to the way someone may have felt when they were saved.

Early on they had the joy of being forgiven, the relief of escaping eternal damnation, the hope of a

"First love happens when we find in another what is desperately needed in ourselves."

new beginning; in other words, a clean slate. A combination of these provided somewhat of a spiritual "honeymoon" which for some reason cooled over time. So the idea I had before was that I needed to go back to those early "feelings" when I first "fell in love" with Jesus. That idea doesn't work for me for several reasons.

1. Feelings can't drive the spiritual train. The fact of Scriptura; truth must inform our spirits which then encourages our hearts in love toward Jesus.
2. Feelings were not a major part in my conversion. It was more of a surrender of my will to Him!
3. I love Jesus more today than I ever have. I don't want to go back. In fact, if done right, the Christian life centered in God's Word and understanding should cause our love for Jesus to increase over time. Growing in grace and knowledge is a treasure that constantly awards unending dividends.

So, what is first love? Here's my definition.

First love happens when we find in another what is desperately needed in ourselves. And the greater the desperation, the greater the appreciation and adoration. There is no greater demonstration of this than the scene at the cross. It was a show-down. Three major doctrinal realities converge at the cross.

1. The holiness of God accompanied with all of its perfect justice, its all-consuming fire and wrath.
2. The total depravity of man accompanied with its clear demonstration of rebellion and ignorance.
3. The unconditional love, mercy and forgiveness of God as His innocent Lamb is willingly caught in the thicket for us!

Fast forward to the most vulnerable day of our lives when we will stand before His holiness. What will our "felt-need" be? It will be to be robed in appreciation throughout eternity with an attitude of first love knowing first-hand how desperate we really were. That desperation needs to be studied in the Scriptures, reviewed in our fellowship and demonstrated in our lifestyle of worship.

What are First Works?

A picture is worth a thousand words, so picture the scene of the sinful woman who crushed the Pharisee's arrogance when he invited Jesus to dinner (Luke 7:36-50). Twice Luke relates in the narrative that she was a noted sinner. Her worship was described as follows: "And behold, a woman in the city, which was a sinner, when she knew that Jesus sat at meat in the Pharisee's house, brought an alabaster box of ointment, and stood at His feet behind Him weeping, and began to wash His feet with tears, and did wipe them with the hairs of her head, and kissed His feet, and anointed them with the ointment" (v. 37, 38). Luke's description of her actions and the intensity of the verbs used here lets us know that she made a scene to express her desperate need and loving appreciation. As leaders we must cultivate this kind of worship as the lifestyle of our church.

Expressions may vary, but our hearts should be hot with love. Jesus observed the bewilderment of the Pharisee and engaged him in a dialogue in which He explained the difference between the Pharisee's lack of respect for Jesus and the sinful woman's lavish gestures, i.e., the Pharisee's rationalizing his deep need of forgiveness while the sinful woman seemingly recognized her need for forgiveness. Jesus summarized His analysis of the situation with this, "To whom little is forgiven the same loveth little" (v. 47). A good servant-leader is always reminding himself and those he leads of how much they have been forgiven. From this story, I would suggest that the "first works" Jesus seeks in believers is a heart condition reflecting our deep need of Him in the light of the blazing holiness of God and the *relief* experienced having learned that Jesus paid it all. My heart leaps afresh as I write this. Roy Hession says, **"The gospel is good news for bad people."** That should make us worship and turn every act of service into a sweet gesture of thanksgiving. From the example of this woman, let me suggest three practices that may partially describe the place to which Jesus would like us to return.

"A good servant-leader is always reminding himself and those he leads of how much they have been forgiven."

1. Honest humble repentance. The Lord sees repenters as those who worship Him with the ongoing admission of their need.
2. Demonstrative faith. The Lord sees believers as those who worship Him with ongoing trust in Christ as their only hope.

3. Extravagant thanksgiving. The Lord sees givers as those who take every opportunity to worship with obedient acts of service and sacrifice as an ongoing expression of gratefulness. They have moved from dead works of obligation to the fragrance of adoration.

If we are going to cooperate with Jesus as He fills the church with His life, we must teach our people this style of worship. This is the heart of worship and it goes much deeper than the emotions we experience over a favorite style of music.

Revelation chapter 5 puts this entire idea in context where we see God on the throne with the title deed of the universe in His right hand. He instructs a strong angel to ask a question that paralyzes everyone.

"Who is worthy to open the book, and loose the seals thereof" (v. 2)? No one spoke, no one was able to open the book, or even look at it. John wept much as everyone stood silent with shamed faces. One elder broke the silence, comforted their hearts, and introduced Jesus by calling Him, "The Lion of the tribe of Judah, the Root of David" who hath prevailed to open the book and to loose the seven seals thereof." The "Slain Lamb" appeared in the middle of the throne and took the book so that God's plan for the ages would move forward. If we let our biblical imagination work here, we realize this is a breath-taking moment. At that point, everyone celestial and everyone terrestrial yet redeemed begins to worship. New songs of worthiness and redemption burst forth.

"Worthy is the Lamb that was slain to receive power, and riches, and wisdom, and strength, and honour, and glory, and blessing" (v. 12). This is the perfect revelation of the first-love worship of the sufficiency of Christ, and we must do our best to imitate it in our churches. If this scene of heavenly beings reveals such thankfulness, how much more should we on earth feel the need to respond in like manner?

How do we lead our congregations to revive and maintain their first love? By reminding ourselves of the ongoing intentional focus on the person and cross-work of Jesus Christ. Jesus Himself gave the church a way to do this when He instituted the Lord's Supper.

And He took bread and gave thanks, and broke it, and gave unto them saying, 'This is My body which is given for you; this do in REMEMBRANCE of Me.' Likewise also the cup after supper, saying, 'This cup is the New Testament in My blood, which is shed for you. –Luke 22:19-20

The Lord knows how prone we are to forget the gravity of our lostness and the sacrifice for our salvation, so He built in a simple yet significant way for us to be reminded. I have found the more intense church life becomes, the more frequent the Lord's Supper should be practiced.

At times it should be made a priority of the day, the center piece of the worship event. When Paul reviews this with the Corinthian church, he emphasizes the word "remembrance." He also clearly states that, "As often as ye eat this bread, and drink this cup, ye do shew the Lord's death till He come" (I Corinthians 11:26). He knew that the best way to remember was to review again and again until Jesus returns.

Paul also spoke of the attitudes to be displayed during this time of remembrance. Respectfulness (v. 27), self-examination (v. 28), reverence, fear of God and discernment (v. 29-30) all create a sacred biblical moment as we pause in quietness remembering the Lamb at Calvary. Make these moments a priority as often as you are led. An intentional review of the past can help sanctify the present and set us on course for future ministry. These are times when you as a leader can call your ministry to a stop and give everyone a chance to tell Jesus of their love. Your people are constantly fighting the rush of "the everyday" and will benefit greatly from these sacred breaks. Give your congregation "Selah" moments for remembrance and reflection. You may have to trim your message and cut some music, but the benefits will protect you from Jesus coming and shutting the ministry down completely! We have authority through Jesus to defeat the attacks of Satan, but when Jesus sets His face against us, we will be gone (Revelation 2:5).

In summary, the loving worship of Jesus can never be separate from the understanding of Scripture. The Bible does allow us to have objective truth (logos) and subjective reality (rhema), but we will never enjoy first-love in our spirits without the Word of God.

When Jesus met the woman at the well (John 4), He said to her that the Father was seeking true worshipers (v. 23). In His dialogue with her, He exposed three categories of worshipers:

1. Ignorant worshipers
   "Ye worship ye know not what" (v. 22a).
2. Knowledgeable worshipers
   "We know what we worship" (v. 22b).
3. True worshipers
   "But the hour cometh and now is, when the true worshipers shall worship the Father in spirit and in truth"; (v. 23)

That's our goal. In this stewardship, we must lead our flock to become true worshipers who love Jesus through obedience and adoration.

From Belief to Behavior:
- Make much of the Lord's supper.
- Take time to remember, repent and return.
- Remember obedience is God's love language.
- Use words like "in love" with Jesus.
- Sing to Him (no performances please).
- Write love letters to Him together.
- Worship Jesus with your sermons (Pastors).

Reality #27—The Stewardship of Warfare

Finally, brethren, be strong in the Lord and the power of His might. –Ephesians 6:10

Thou, therefore, my son, be strong in the grace that is in Christ Jesus. –II Timothy 2:1

The authority/sufficiency of Christ is tried and proven in the oven of adversity (The Stewardship of Adversity).

Our Stewardship: To fight (agonize) the good fight of faith (I Timothy 6:12).

This verse from Paul's instruction to young Timothy was used in both military and athletic endeavors to describe the concentration, discipline, and extreme effort needed to win. The "good fight of faith" is the spiritual conflict with Satan's kingdom of darkness in which all men of God are necessarily involved. We do not wrestle against flesh and blood (Ephesians 6:12), we do not war according to the flesh (II Corinthians 10:3), and our weapons of warfare are not carnal (human) but mighty in God for pulling down strongholds (II Corinthians 10:4). In a word, the Bible clearly says our enemies are not flesh, our war is not a flesh effort, and our weapons are not human! But when our church is fighting, all we encounter seems to be flesh! We read body language, see angry faces, hear cutting words and watch the hallway huddles that curb their conversation when we walk near. All these signs of flesh give us suspicions about the war with the darkness. Let me say it simply and clearly, "A good steward of revival must not be surprised when adversity comes." Adversity is as much

"A good steward of revival must not be surprised when adversity comes."

a part of life with the Vine as grace and faith and worship. Remember, Jesus our Lead Pastor was led by the Spirit into the wilderness to be tempted of the Devil (Matthew 4:1). What our enemy intends for evil our Father turns for good in the long run. Many a church has been caught off guard, discouraged, disillusioned and defeated because they thought the reviving of God was a cure-all—the end of all problems. Remember also that trials come from without and from within. The ones from within are the most hurtful and surprising.

Peter helps us here, "Beloved, think it not strange concerning the fiery trial which is to try you, as though some strange thing happened unto you" (I Peter 4:12).

In seamless fashion he continues to equip the believer with six attitudes that will enable him to endure and employ the fire.

1. Expect it (v. 12).
2. Rejoice in it (v. 13, 14).
3. Evaluate the cause (v. 15-18).
4. Entrust it to God (v. 19).
5. Feed the flock with truth (5:2).
6. Take oversight willingly (5:2).

You must lead your flock to do the same. Fighting each other is not an option. Remaining objective when under fire is one of the toughest challenges of ministry. Don't fight alone. Two are always better than one and a threefold cord is not quickly broken (Ecclesiastes 4:9-12).

Lead Pastor

"Remaining objective when under fire is one of the toughest challenges of ministry."

A pastor should always be in the process of enlarging his intimate prayer team and building a team-type ministry. There is a reason why Jesus sent the 70 out 2x2 and why He called Paul and Barnabas and why Paul only traveled alone once. Paul's missionary journeys were, for the most part, a team effort. In a multitude of counselors there is safety (Proverbs 15:22; 24:6).

Ellen S. Lister selected quotes from the letters of Samuel Rutherford (1600-1661) and put them together in a tiny book entitled "The Loveliness of Christ." Many of his letters were an encouragement to ministers who were suffering adversity. Two quotes are helpful to us here.

"I found it most true, that the greatest temptation out of hell is to live without temptation; grace withereth without adversity. The devil is but God's master fencer, to teach us to handle our weapons."

A reviving from God is not the end of all battles but rather an equipping for battles. The sovereign working of God in revival will prepare us for the sovereignly approved visitation of trials. That's why stewardship of adversity is so important. God is not about protecting us from all warfare but rather providing us with mighty weapons for warfare."

Rutherford's second quote introduces another dimension of adversity that is often overlooked. i.e., the ways of God. "My shallow and ebb thoughts are not the compass Christ saileth by. I leave His ways to Himself, for they are far, far above me. There are windings and *tos* and *fros* in His ways, which blind bodies like us cannot see." Dear friend, please remember we are living with the vibrant, lovely and life-giving Vine whose ways are past finding out (Romans 11:33). Don't be surprised by the windings, the reverses or the quietness. My friend Andy Harkleroad reminds us, "The Teacher is silent during the test, but He is not absent." He is building His church even when we can't imagine it.

When hard times come, we often forget the splendor of God's ways. He knows that grace grows best in winter. Isaiah captured it in classic fashion.

For My thoughts are not your thoughts, neither are your ways My ways, saith the Lord. For as the heavens are higher than the earth, so are My ways higher than your ways, and My thoughts your thoughts. –Isaiah 55:8-9

My life changed in 1974 when I heard Bill Gothard (Basic Life Institute) teach about the ways of God. His instruction at that time was for us to note this sequence in Scripture.

1. God starts with a vision followed by a —
2. Death of a vision then possibly a —
3. Double death of a vision then a —
4. Supernatural fulfillment of the vision.

Abraham is an icon of this. God's promise to Abraham being a great nation was followed by a barren womb which then produced the promised child in old age. All of our faith heroes experienced "Death Valley Days" so that God would get all the glory. Again, our Lead Pastor not only wants us to learn God's Word and do God's will, He wants us to learn God's ways and grow.

The temptation for us during those days is to either quit or take matters into our own hands. Neither option is good stewardship. Abraham's choice to go into Hagar left some serious side effects. The point here is that our ministry may have to go backward before it goes forward. When it does, don't defect and don't manipulate. This is a time to be still, be obedient and let patience have her perfect work. Remember this is not a book about "How to do it." Leading your flock responsibly through God-ordained adversity is an art learned at the hand of the Father. He is the faithful husbandman of the vine-branch relationship. He knows how to purge and prop every branch for maximum fruit. While on a mission in Southern France, I was astonished at how brutally the vinedressers trimmed the vines in order to experience a greater harvest. Sometimes it's extremely hard to know what's going on. But don't panic. Just stay faithful.

Here's a faith-cycle you may notice in your ministry. Turbulent winds, if responded to properly, can help our lives and ministries to soar higher. It's like setting our sail to catch the wind. It's like an eagle who soars higher because of the storm. Even the Wright Brothers remind us that, "Birds don't soar in a calm."

Here's a common scenario of turbulence:

1. We experience a lack of threat or need which causes—
2. An inner disturbance in which we—
3. Yield our will—we surrender to God.
4. There is momentary affirmation.
5. Followed by deeper despair calling for greater trust which is rewarded by. (This could be that "double death of a vision".)

6. An inner rest and inner supply which frees us to—
7. Analyze the situation.
8. Birth a plan of action.
9. Take faith-sized steps.

"If you lead your ministry to ride the winds of turbulence, you will be a faithful steward."

This cycle is evenly divided into three parts in which we choose (1-3), trust (4-6) and act (7-9). This is a very common cycle used by the faithful servants of Scripture. Moses, for instance, chose to suffer with the people of God (Hebrews 11:25). He trusted God with a long, rollercoaster-type of experience (Hebrews 11:27) until he marched with 1.5 million people out of Egypt (Hebrews 11:29). We revere his endurance to the end as he lived out God's calling on his life. If you lead your ministry to ride the winds of turbulence, you will be a faithful steward.

This same pattern is seen in the Apostle Paul's first missionary journey (Acts 13, 14). In Cyprus, Antioch and Iconium the same sequence appears.

1. Communication
2. Opposition
3. Perseverance
4. Fruit
5. Glory

It should be comforting to us to know that this great steward of the mysteries of God (I Corinthians 4:1) also faced great opposition in the process of being faithful. The writer of Hebrews reminds us that, if we find ourselves wearied and faint in our minds, we must fix our eyes on Jesus who endured the contradiction of sinners like no one else. Through perfect obedience He earned the right to be set down at the right hand of the Throne of God.

Let me conclude this reality with a Scripture that will launch us into our next stewardship. God is working through adversity in order to do you, as a leader, a favor. Listen to this from Paul, "…I hear that there be divisions among you and I partly believe it. For there must be also heresies among you, that they which are approved may be made manifest among you (I Corinthians 11:18,19).

Factions and adversity often reveal those who have passed the test of spiritual genuineness and purity. We will not be able to take the mixed multitude to maturity. "Curious onlookers" and "bread and fish" followers do not make the cut during adversity. Through trials, the "cream" rises to the top and the faithful remnant will appear. Honestly, I have often been surprised at who endures through hard times. Again, in the ministry of Jesus, "Many of His disciples went back and walked no more with Him after some hard teachings (John 6:66). The residual effect of a faithful stewardship during adversity will leave you with a committed remnant who will then follow Jesus by choice.

From Belief to Behavior:
- Enlarge your prayer closet with trusted comrades.
- List the trials and give thanks for them
  (I Thessalonians 5:18).
  (An exercise in picking up the shield of faith)
- Lay down all pride and identify areas of deficiency—
  and learn.
- Turn your eyes upon Jesus (Hebrews 12:1-3).
  (Engage His sufficiency).

Reality #28—Choice/Discipleship

And the things that thou hast heard of Me among many witnesses, the same commit thou to faithful men, who shall be able to teach others. –Ephesians 6:10

The authority/reality of Christ becomes clearly focused when we count the cost and make a choice.

<u>Our Stewardship:</u> To disciple the faithful who will teach others.

By grace, through faith, in worship and in warfare, you should now begin to identify those who are being faithful in attitude and actions. They are to be discipled, trained, and commissioned. This is where we begin to multiply shepherds. When I started ministry, discipleship was not emphasized; but I had a sense that new converts needed to be "followed up" and in a short time there was not enough of "me" to go around. I started discipling in random manner just to survive. Now it's my way of life for ministry, and I find it delightful to watch the multiplication process take place. Making disciples is not a cookie-cutter process. Some grow faster than others. Different backgrounds will require varying approaches etc., but the principle is the same; that is, train the faithful in ministry that is suited for their personality and calling. **If your ministry is to stay healthy, while you grow in numbers, then you must grow in good shepherds amongst the flock.**

Any reviving can experience some "fall out" which can be discouraging to you and disheartening to those who watch. The timid ones as well as the skeptics may try to discredit

"Multiply the faithful and you will multiply your ministry." what God is doing, but you can be strong in grace and commit to the faithful your philosophy and approach to ministry. Their growth and passion will be a securing factor for the long haul and lay to rest the fear of others. For the most part I have found that the "net" result of revival in a local ministry is a faithful remnant who have had their awareness of the crucified life and the filling of the Spirit raised. They have counted the cost and made the choice to follow Jesus at any cost. With no hidden expectations, no personal agenda, and no double-mindedness they follow. They are rewarded with a growing reality in their relationship with Him which only serves to cause them to hunger for more. These deserve our priority attention. For years I tried to keep the unfaithful in church while neglecting those faithful ones who always stayed by the Lord. **Multiply the faithful and you will multiply your ministry.**

There are many good resources today on how to do discipleship. You can research them and decide what approach best fits your situation. Just know that it's God's instruction to us and then get at it. There is no perfect, end-all method. Start doing life together and talk as you go along. Hands-on training coupled with Bible examination are great at any level and there are many levels. Some disciples can hardly unpack John 3:16 while others are well advanced in information but simply lacking in application. You will have to sort out where you start and stop with each one. Don't be afraid to get dirty and don't be intimidated by those smarter than you. A great teacher makes the student think he knows more than the teacher.

Older to Younger

Don't forget that older teaching the younger is a very natural and effective way of commissioning the faithful and multiplying shepherds. Older, Spirit-filled believers who have weathered the storms of life make tremendous mentors. With the breakdown of the family, these folks provide surrogate dads and moms for the young who are raising their children. My dad's advice to me has paid unmeasurable dividends in ministry. He told me again and again, "Joe, respect your elders, you will be old someday." I have heeded his advice, which is Scriptural, and have treated the older men as fathers and the older women as mothers. They have not only encouraged my life and family but have participated in ministry as well. It is my practice to give value to all ages which, in turn, opens their hearts to learning and growing. With this attitude on your part, you will discover the wisdom of the sage who has the freshness of youth. The key is discerning Spirit-filledness.

Paul was very bold to make this idea of the older teaching the younger a part of sound doctrine as well as a practical training dynamic which protects the Word of God from being blasphemed (Titus 2:1-5). The reviving life of Christ is well-served by these aging friends. This encouragement goes far deeper than slapping backs and goofy cliché talk. This is wisdom with "skin on", reaching out in loving relationships. Your discipleship role here is to help each one to identify the gifts he or she owns that will well serve the younger part of the flock. This will give them dignity and fresh purpose. You may have to craft a ministry vehicle to get them started.

Live in a Discipleship Sandwich

Teach your congregation to live in a II Timothy 2:2 sandwich like Timothy. He was to be accountable to Paul and responsible for faithful men. If everyone will align themselves under a faithful person to whom they are accountable and pray to find God's person for whom they are responsible, disciples will multiply exponentially. I love to watch it happen.

The Road from Saul to Paul

It may help us to observe the Lord's sanctification process as He transformed Saul the terrorist into Paul the evangelist and church planter. It was not a straight line, nor a gentle slope upward. Every discipleship effort has some surprises. Notice these classic stages in Paul's life on the road to becoming God's apostle to the Gentiles (Acts 9:13):

Stage 1–Repentance and Faith (Acts 9:1-17)

First, there is a changed life. Repentance and faith are two sides of the same coin and they both become the lifestyle of the Kingdom. Someone who is not willing to change cannot be discipled.

Stage 2–Enlightenment (Acts 9:17, 18)

This is where the disciple learns about the One who made the change. Because Paul learned this so well up front, he was able to boldly say throughout his ministry, "For I am not ashamed of the gospel of Christ; for it is the power of God unto salvation to everyone that believeth: to the Jew first and also to the Greek" (Romans 1:16).

<u>Stage 3–Ministry Training</u> (Acts. 9:19, 20)
This is basic involvement when the disciple observes and participates in a limited way with others in kingdom work. Various servant roles provide a good entry level for learning.

<u>Stage 4–Leadership Development</u> (Acts 9:21, 22)
During this stage, participation in ministry becomes consistent, and leadership qualities and giftedness begin to surface. People around them begin to comment on the difference. This was especially true in Saul's case (v. 21). Saul increased in strength and his conviction about Christ coupled with his reasoning mind made him a ready defender, confounding the Jews and proving that Jesus was in fact the Christ. This was happening without a lot of coaching from others. A good point to be made here is that when people are truly convicted by God and saved by God, are counting the cost of following God, and are hearing from God, they will increase with the fullness of God (Ephesians 3:19). They are a joy to watch. Love, encourage, and protect them because the next stage may not be so easy.

<u>Stage 5–Separation and Re-evaluation</u>
Leadership in God's work demands time and testing to prove authenticity and breaking of the vessel (Acts 9:23-31). The making of a minister is similar to the making of a ministry. Both are branch-like, abiding in the Vine, to be purged by the husbandman Father (John 15:2). Saul was a "hot potato" and needed some time to find his balance. The Jews were trying to kill him (v. 23), and the disciples were afraid of him (v. 26). Barnabas became his advocate before the apostles (v. 27). While with the apostles in Jerusalem, he began disputing against the

"The reward of disciple-making is the call of God." Grecians who in turn tried to slay him (v. 29). The brethren finally brought him down to Caesarea and sent him forth to Tarsus (v. 30). At this point, Paul disappeared from prominent ministry for several years, although he possibly founded some churches around Syria and Cilicia (Galatians 1:21).

Depending on the circumstances, **God knows how to move His disciple around for their ongoing growth and refinement.**

Stage 6–Leadership in Ministry (Acts 11:25, 26)

Here the leader leads. It is now time for the disciple-in-progress to practice the decisions he made in his time of testing. By now he can teach from both knowledge and experience. He now relates with the attitude of brokenness and dependence.

Stage 7–World Vision

This is now a maturity that is open to God's sovereign placement (Acts 13:1-3). I love this moment described here. "As they ministered to the Lord, and fasted the Holy Ghost said, 'Separate Me Barnabas and Saul for the work whereunto I have called them.' And when they had fasted and prayed, they laid their hands on them, they sent them away" (Acts 13:2, 3).

The reward of disciple-making is the call of God. Some are called to stay with us, and some are called to go elsewhere. Either way, we are multiplying ministry and building His church. Steward well. Like the apostle Paul, growing disciples often get their start within.

Reality #29—The Stewardship of Body Life

And He gave some apostles; and some, prophets; and some evangelists; and some pastors and teachers, for the perfecting of the saints, for the work of the ministry, for the edifying of the body of Christ. –Ephesians 4:11-12

The reality of Christ permeates the true church as the body ministers to itself in love (The Stewardship of Body Life).

<u>Our Stewardship:</u> To equip the saints within the local body to live and serve in harmony and to edify one another in love (Ephesians 4:16).

The reviving life of the Vine thrives in an atmosphere of love where people are laying down their lives for their friends. Our job as shepherds is to equip them to minister to each other. This chapter is different from the previous one in that while discipleship is focused on the growth of the individual, this stewardship focuses on the health of the whole body.

I was introduced to the concept of equipping the saints when I was thirty, just prior to starting my relationship with our second church. Before that I basically understood myself to be a preacher, teacher, soul winner, visitation pastor, and activity director. I was your typical "one-man band." Again, it was all I knew. My beloved seminary professor and predecessor in our second church, Dr. Gerry Benn, shared this concept with me, and my ministry life took on a whole new adventure. The Bible says that the pastor is Christ's gift to the church to equip the saints for the work of ministry. I resisted this truth at first because I feared the delegation of ministry would be interpreted as laziness on my part. However, when our people saw the effect of many hands and felt the joy of ownership and my trust in them, they formed a great team to minister with intention. I like to think of it like coaching. Help each member to assess his or her gifts and callings, train him or her in how to use those gifts in the body, and then plug each individual into practical ministry within the body to serve one another. I suggest you familiarize yourself with the motivational gifts of Romans 12 and then lead members to identify which ones best describe their heart throb for ministry. Here's what each heart-gift might relate if you asked them what they were looking for in a church. I actually was taught these at the *Institute of Basic Life Principles* advanced seminar one year after I realized I needed to equip my flock. God has always provided just what I needed at just the right time.

Here's the list of gifts in order with their emphasis.

<u>Prophets:</u> Look for well-prepared sermons exposing sin, proclaiming righteousness, and warning of judgment to come.

<u>Servers:</u> Look for practical assistant to each member of the church to encourage him and to help him fulfill his responsibilities.

<u>Teachers:</u> Look for in-depth Bible studies with special emphasis on precise meaning of words.

<u>Exhorters:</u> Look for personal counseling and encouragement for each member to assist him in applying scriptural principles to his daily living.

<u>Givers:</u> Look for generous programs of financial assistance to missionaries and other ministries.

Administrators: Look for smooth-running organizations throughout the church so that every phase will be carried out decently and in order.

"Ministry happens when divine resources meet human needs through loving channels for the glory of God."

Mercy Showers: Look for special outreach and concern for the precise and varying feelings of individuals with a readiness to meet their needs.

While an attitude of serving should prevail at all times, knowledge of specific giftedness and motivation helps the servant enjoy the journey more and bring maximum benefit to all. Warren Wiersbe says, "Ministry happens when divine resources meet human needs through loving channels for the glory of God." God is always the source, but loving channels properly placed are a God-send to the body. You can never be everything to everybody, but the body working together becomes the fullness of Christ in your midst. Again, quoting Wiersbe, "We are not manufacturers, we are only distributors." A good pastor learns how to distribute the gifts God has given. This stewardship of body life also relates to the first two stewardships of grace and faith.

For I say, through the grace given unto me, to every man that is among you, not to think of himself more highly than he ought to think, but to think soberly, according as God hath dealt to every man the measure of faith. For as we have many members in one body, and all members have not the same office: So we being many are one body in Christ, and everyone members one of another.
–Romans 12:3-5

"Revival thrives best where doctrinal stability secures the foundation."

Paul lists five qualitative goals that flow from a body that effectively edifies itself in love (Ephesians 4:13-16):

1. Unity of the faith (v. 13a)
    This is a unity of confidence in the character of God as well as a unity in transforming gospel doctrine.

2. Christlikeness of believers (v. 13b)
    This is a church with members that are becoming like the "Perfect One." They are approaching the measure of the stature of the fullness of Christ.

3. Stability of believers (v. 14)
    These are Christians who know what they believe and why. We especially need this in our postmodern, post Christian subjective-truth culture. Every worldview must be accountable for its own interpretation. When I started pastoring 50 years ago, the landscape of the culture looked quite different. Many of my younger disciples are actually coaching me in the changes in today's mindset—another example of the ministry of the body even to its pastor. Changing winds of doctrine should not blow us off course. Revival thrives best where doctrinal stability secures the foundation.

4. <u>Truthing in love</u> (v. 15)
    This is a literal translation of the original. Speaking the truth in love is an indication of growing up into Christ our head. When our confidence in God is strong, then Christlikeness dominates our attitude, and our doctrine is secure. It becomes us, then, to be able to speak the truth in love. Truthing in love serves the gospel well whether we are witnessing to the lost, correcting our children, or confronting our peers with sensitive issues. The life of the Vine flows freely through this quality of the branch.

5. <u>Harmony of the Body</u> (v. 16)
    Here we see that Christ makes the whole body fit together by flowing through each member as he or she does his or her part, thus helping other parts to grow so that the whole body is healthy and growing in full love.

Pastor, if you're like me you would rejoice to see this happening in your church. At this point, equipping the saints for ministry should look pretty valuable to us.

Our Lead Pastor not only role-modeled this for us by equipping His own disciples, but He considers us as His gift to the church to do the same.

One Another

The life of the Vine freely flows amongst the branches as we embrace our call and commitment to the "one another" commands of scripture, both positive and negative. Don't overlook the Holy Spirit's curriculum for supernatural body life. Lead your flock to carefully consider the dynamic of each one as it is fleshed out in a real world. Imagine how a newcomer feels when he or she comes into an atmosphere where these are in place. Here's a sample of them.

Romans 12:10:
Be kindly affectionate one to another with brotherly love; in honour preferring one another.
(God's way of giving significance and defending the gospel).

Romans 12:16:
Be of the same mind one to another.
(God's way of developing fellowships).

Romans 15:7:
Wherefore receive ye one another, as Christ also received us to the glory of God.
(God's way of showing acceptance).

Romans 15:14:
And I myself also am persuaded of you, my brethren, that ye also are full of goodness, filled with all knowledge, able also to admonish one another.
(Paul was encouraged that they could minister intelligently to one another.)

Galatians 5:13:
For, brethren, ye have been called into liberty; only use not liberty for an occasion to the flesh, but by love serve one another.
(The freedom of liberty provides the energy to serve other believers.)

Galatians 6:1, 2:

Brethren, if a man be overtaken in a fault, ye which are spiritual restore such an one in the spirit of meekness: considering thyself, lest thou also be tempted. Bear ye one another's burdens, and so fulfill the law of Christ.

(Here, even the restoration of a fallen brother is a team effort of body life).

Ephesians 4:32:

And be ye kind one to another, tenderhearted, forgiving one another, even as God for Christ's sake hath forgiven you.

(Kindness and forgiveness are major components to loving, long-term relationships).

Hebrews 3:13:

But exhort one another daily, while it is call Today; lest any of you be hardened through the deceitfulness of sin.

(The pastor doesn't have to be the only one who confronts and encourages).

James 5:16:

Confess your faults one to another, and pray one for another, that ye may be healed. The effectual fervent prayer of a righteous man availeth much.

(Healing physically and spiritually through honest confession before trusted friends and prayer breeds revival in the church).

<u>I Peter 4:9, 10:</u>
Use hospitality one to another without grudging. As every man hath received the gift, even so minister the same one to another, as good stewards of the manifold grace of God.
(In a broken world, generosity ministered through hospitality gives a feeling of home and security to needy souls).

Think of it. If these ten dynamics were functioning in our churches through Spirit-filled believers, the reality of the life of Christ would be evident. In this context we model Jesus with skin on; incarnate!

This kind of love draws true believers back to the assembly to enjoy the presence of Christ. The assembly of "freed up" believers is unselfish and contagious. This is a worthy stewardship for any pastor to teach, train and model.

Reality #30—Evangelism

And they, continuing daily with one accord in the temple, and breaking bread from house to house, did eat their meat with gladness and singleness of heart, praising God, and having favour with all the people. And the Lord added to the church daily such as should be saved. –Acts 2:46, 47

Without fail I hear pastors express concern about their congregations not being evangelistic. Where do we start in nurturing them to overflow with the life and message of Jesus? Our Lead Pastor started with instruction that resulted in fullness of joy (John 15:11).

Help Their Joy

How often I heard Ralph and Lou Sutera of the Canadian Revival Fellowship say, "When revival is the experience of the church, then evangelism will be the expression of the church." Del Fehsenfeld, the founder of Life Action Ministries, said the same thing from a different direction. "Some believers wouldn't wish their Christianity on their worst enemy." In agreement, John Piper says, "People who prize Jesus praise Jesus." He continues, "Missions exist because worship doesn't." Nehemiah of old said to his workers, "The joy of the Lord is your strength" (Nehemiah 8:10). One of my favorite messages during our Sutera ministry was entitled, "Joy is the Serious Business of Heaven." The Psalmist queried, "Wilt thou be angry with us forever? Wilt thou draw thine anger to all generations? Wilt thou not revive us again; that thy people may rejoice in thee?" (Psalm 85:5, 6).

> *"We who serve or lead should not go very long without our 'song'."*

Our stewardship of shepherding should result in the saints enjoying such reality in Christ that they minister out of the overflow of a full heart. I realize that life is not always "happy—happy—happy." BUT we are instructed to "Let the Word of Christ dwell in you richly in all wisdom; teaching and admonishing one another in psalms and hymns and spiritual songs, singing with grace in your hearts to the Lord" (Colossians 3:16). An essential part of the witness of our lives in and out of the church is joy. I love to say that singing is not for those who have a voice but for those who have a "song." We who serve or lead should not go very long without our "song." Sheep feel secure with a joyful shepherd whose habit is only to be angry with the wolves. Paul related his heart to the problem-ridden church at Corinth, "Moreover I call God as witness against my soul, that to spare you I came no more to Corinth. Not that we have dominion over your faith, but are fellow workers for your joy; for by faith you stand" (II Corinthians 1:23, 24) NKJV.

With God as witness Paul said.

1. I gave you time and space to repent.
2. I have no interest in domination.
3. I am a helper of our joy.

In this stewardship of evangelism, we are right to start with being helpers and models of joy. Countless times over my 50 years of ministry, I have had to find a place to retreat for a while, and like David, encourage myself in the Lord.

Satan hates the spreading of the gospel, and leadership that helps move people toward a joyful, bold witness of the gospel will often come under attack. In David's case at Ziklag, the women and children had been taken captive, the city had been burned with fire, his army wept till they could weep

"...unified, glad and single-hearted believers make the best evangelists."

no more, and some spoke of stoning David. Alone with God, David found encouragement and direction from God to win a great battle and recover all that the Amalekites had taken (I Samuel 30). Sometimes, you will have to fight for your joy as well.

From the autobiography of George Mueller we read, "It has pleased the Lord to teach me a truth, the benefit of which I have not lost for more than 14 years. The point is this: I saw more clearly than ever the first great and primary business to which I ought to attend every day was to have my soul happy in the Lord. The first thing to be concerned about was not how much I might serve the Lord, or how I might glorify the Lord but how I might get my soul into a happy state, and how my inner man might be nourished.

"How different, when the soul is refreshed and made happy early in the morning, from what it is when, without spiritual preparation, the service, the trials, and the temptations of the day come upon me!"[10]

People are more likely to follow a joyful leader.

In short, unified, glad and single-hearted believers make the best evangelists. They seem to find favor with people, and doors seem to open for them. The Lord loves to add new babies to these joyful nurseries (Acts 2:46, 47).

Pray in the Harvest

Don't miss Jesus' way of keeping people passionate for the harvest. Notice the progression of these familiar words, "The harvest truly is plenteous but the labourers are few; Pray ye therefore the Lord of the harvest, that He will send forth labourers into His harvest" (Matthew 9:37, 38). This is Christ's way of making our church excellent at outreach. He first wants us, through prayer, to become occupied with the Lord of the harvest. When we do, He pours His life and passion for the shepherdless multitude into us. As we follow Him, He sends us forth into strategic places with sufficient power. While there, we freely give away what He has freely given to us (Matthew 10:1-8). We never need to evangelize in our own limited strength. We can live by His life and be empowered by His passion for the harvest. The secret to keeping people reaching out is to keep them reaching up. Jesus is still "moved with compassion", literally "sick to His stomach" over the multitudes. So He instructs us, "Abide in Me, and I in you. As the branch cannot bear fruit of itself, except it abide in the Vine; no more can ye, except ye abide in Me. I am the Vine, Ye are the branches; He that abideth in Me and I in him, the same bringeth forth much fruit; for without Me ye can do nothing" (John 15:4,5).

Without the life-giving Vine, the most enthusiastic branch will have a very short ministry. As stewards of evangelism, we need to encourage our branches to abide in the Vine, and lasting fruit will come. (John 15:11)

So far, I have presented the idea that we shepherds must minister to the hearts of the sheep so that their hearts will minister through their mouths and proclaim the good news of Jesus. Mark Dever says, "Evangelism, in other words, is not doing everything we can to get a person to make a decision for Jesus—attempting to force a spiritual birth—. Furthermore,

"The secret to keeping people reaching out is to keep them reaching up."

evangelism is not the same thing as sharing a personal testimony. It's not the same thing as presenting a rational defense of faith. It's not even doing works of charity, though all three of these things may accompany evangelism. Nor should evangelism be confused with the results of evangelism, as if to say we've only successfully evangelized when a conversion follows. No, evangelism is speaking words. It's sharing news. It's being faithful to God by presenting the good news—that Christ, by His death and resurrection has secured a way for a holy God and sinful people to be reconciled. God will produce true conversion when we present this good news. In short, evangelism is presenting the good news freely and trusting God to convert people. Salvation comes from the Lord."

I have strongly felt that part of my stewardship at this point is to stay alert to local opportunities for evangelism and bring them to the attention of the congregation. I like to "scout" things out for them, knowing that prepared hearts will look on their own. Sometimes your approval or caution will encourage them to move out more freely. Here are some common ideas.

1. Teach them to build redemptive relationships with unbelievers.
2. Teach them to use their homes as gospel centers.
3. Give some training in how to give a clear gospel witness.
4. Cast a vision for outreach events where the gospel will be preached. Team evangelism lets even the timid have a part.

5. Teach them how to be alert to divine encounters where a Christian with a prepared heart encounters a lost one who has had God drawing his heart. This is a sweet experience which encourages alertness.

6. Introduce them to local ministries available and looking for volunteers. (Jail ministry, crises pregnancy centers, rest homes, rescue missions, women's shelters, mentoring programs in schools, etc.). Help them see things and reach out.

7. Ordain elders. Be ready to "lay hands" on the faithful and send them forth.

A true reviving from the life of Christ should eventually move us out of our comfort zone into the multitudes with a full heart and a fervent message that Jesus paid it all.

According to Acts 2:42, the New Testament church believed the same truth (doctrine), they shared the same love (fellowship), they remembered the same gospel (breaking of bread), they were depending on the same source (prayer), and they were committed to the same cause, "To know Christ and make Him known."

Summary—Shaping Our Race

In her book, *Beholding and Becoming*, Ruth Chou Simons succinctly says, "What we chase shapes our race." This book is designed to help the local church chase after Jesus by thinking biblically about the Christ-Church relationship.

Before the foundation of the world God ordained the church, Jesus then bought her with His own blood, and then sent the Holy Spirit to be with her always. To this very hour He "knocks" with a heart to be our first love and welcomed guest.

While church ministry may have many dimensions, it has only one driver—intimacy with Jesus. An acrostic for A.B.I.D.E. as mentioned in John 15 could be "Affectual Biblical Intimacy Drives Everything."

In the gospels we see that Jesus was a master at teaching divine truth in a dinner setting. Most always He arrived as a guest or a servant and ended up as the Host because of His authority or power or wisdom or love. The response to His presence was jaw dropping! That's what we're after in this project—jaw dropping grace displayed in your local church.

Even in the well-meaning gospel culture of the church, there are many subtle substitutes for Jesus which beckon us to the chase and exhaust our resources. What was meant to be grace becomes grudge.

May this work bid us to chase after Christ and allow Him to shape our ministries. From the beginning His heart was to pour His life into His bride. A healthy church heeds His knock and tables well and often with Jesus.

Grace to you,

Joe

Works Cited

[1] John Piper, *When I Don't Desire God*, Crossway, Wheaton, IL 60187, 2004

[2] Oswald Chambers, *If You Will Ask*, Discovery House Publishers, Grand Rapids, MI 49512, 1989

[3] A.W. Tozer, *The Knowledge of the Holy*, Harper Collins, New York, N.Y. 1961

[4] F.J. Hugel, *Bones of His Bone*, CLC Publications, Fort Washington, PA 10934, 2009

[5] O. Hallesby, *Prayer*, Augsburg Publishing House, Minneapolis, MN 55440, 1994

[6] Oliver W. Price, *Pray with Christ Obviously Present and Actively in Charge*, Shepherd's Publishing, Covington, IN 47932, 1999

[7] George Müeller, *The Autobiography of George Müeller*, The Whitaker House, New Kingsinton, PA 15068, 1984

[8] C. J. Miller, *Outgrowing the Ingrown Church*, Zondervan Publishing House, Grand Rapids, MI 49530, 1986

[9]Mark Vroegop, *Dark Cloud,* Deep Mercy, Crossway, Wheaton, IL 60187, 2019

[10]George Müller, *The Autobiography of George Müeller,* Compass Circle, 2019 (reprint)